The Comfortologist

A Physician's Empathetic Perspective on
Compassion, Caring, and Pain Relief

By

Steven Drabek, M.D.

The Comfortologist: A Physician's Empathetic
Perspective on Compassion, Caring, and Pain Relief

Copyright © Steven Drabek, M.D. (2025)

Published by:

This book is dedicated to the patients who I have had the honor of providing care for. They entrusted me with their medical care and gave me their friendship.

Throughout the best and worst of times, my wife, Karen Drabek, was always there, along with our children, Madison and Tyler Drabek. Thank you, Karen. And thank you, Madison and Tyler.

I also dedicate this to Don Murray, M.D., who objectively and skillfully treated me through all my medical complications, and to James Bearden, M.D., who found my esophageal cancer so early. May you Rest in Peace, JB. When I see you again, we will go fishing for sure. Thank You.

Table of Contents

Introduction

L et me be clear right up front: I'm a cynic, and most people know that about me. I am particularly cynical about medicine, and yet I have practiced it for forty years.

The reason for my skepticism? Medicine rests on scientific principles and too many people stop there. It takes a human to apply those principles with all the emotions and heart that implies. So, I may be a cynic, but I'm also the guy digging through the horse manure looking for the pony.

I've been wanting to put a human face to the practice of medicine for many years. I just never knew how best to do that until I started reading the *God Winks* books by SQuire Rushnell. The series tells stories of seemingly random events and coincidences that are anything but. In his stories, Rushnell shows they are actually signposts that can help us successfully navigate our careers, relationships, and interests. He says that by recognizing our "God Winks," we can use the untapped power of coincidence to vastly improve our lives.

I believe I had a God Wink moment when I picked up the first book he wrote and realized that God Winks moments have followed me all my life. In a way, they are my story, including the story of telling my history. It was Rushnell's book that inspired me to disseminate my very human message about medicine by writing this book.

The more of Rushnell's *God Winks* stories I read, the more I could trace back the line of "coincidences" that led me to my calling.

I experienced a God Winks moment early in medical school. I had come home from my classes and turned on the television, as I usually did, to watch *Sanford and Son*, one of my favorite shows. But it was too early and I accidentally tuned in to some sort of hospital drama. Well, I didn't want to watch that, so I turned the TV off, clicking it back on at 3:25 p.m. to catch the tail end of the show where a little girl had just been told that her mother was gone and she couldn't see her.

"No!" the child said. "I'm going to see my mother! I'm going to be with her and I'm going to talk to her!" Shoulders squared, she walked down the long white corridor and opened the door of her mother's room. She walked to the bed and stood by her mother's body, saying her goodbyes.

I was stunned, caught completely off guard by a rush of emotions I couldn't quite name.

Then, one day in 1999, I picked up another one of the *God Winks* books, *God Winks On Love,* that I had purchased for my daughter, who was having relationship issues. I was going through Rushnell's introduction when one paragraph leaped out at me: more than a decade ago, he had produced after-school children's specials for television. One of them was the hospital drama that had so strongly caught my attention.

Like the little girl in the drama, I was six when my mother passed, and I use the word "passed" deliberately because when my father came home from the hospital that night, he told my siblings and me, "Your mother has passed away."

I had no idea what he meant. I wandered down the hall of the friend's house we were staying with and opened the door to their son's bedroom. He was my age and when I asked what my father had meant, he said, "Your mom's gone. She's not coming back."

The shock of his words carved right through my body. How could she be gone? She hadn't been ill, had she? No one had told me she was sick. No one said she was going to have surgery. How could she be okay just yesterday and suddenly be gone forever? Besides, we had just moved into my mother's dream home!

She'd been a much-loved nurse, and hundreds of people came to her funeral, including everyone who had attended school with her or worked with her. At the end of the service, Charles Dowell, the preacher, approached us where we sat in the front pew. "Do you all wish to view the body?" he asked my father.

My father said, "No."

I don't know if I had the coherent thought, "Yes! I want to see her!" but not seeing her left me with a deep sense of emptiness. Years later, when I was in medical school, we attended a presentation by a rather theatrical psychiatrist who talked about the importance of closure. I felt like he had punched me in the gut. I needed closure. I'd been denied that when she passed in the hospital and then again in the church.

Unlike the girl on television, I had never had the chance to say goodbye.

As you read about the God Winks in my life, I hope you realize your life is full of God Winks as well. I have met many people in my work and career who believe their life is unimportant, but I have never met a person whose life didn't matter.

So many people have inspired me by honoring me with the task of caring for them at the end of their lives. Working with hospice, I have experienced the joy of relieving their suffering through the care I provided. The medical community might look at this book with immense skepticism, but most didn't go into medicine for the same reason I did.

I took up medicine to help people, and I have stayed true to that throughout my career, and I have loved my work. I have seen countless God Winks and learned lessons beyond measure.

I should also point out that God has a wicked sense of humor. I suspect He keeps me around because I provide Him with many belly laughs. I'm sure He chuckled gleefully after my esophageal surgery when I found it almost impossible to hold back tears. It bothered me badly at first. Now, I've accepted the fact that real men do cry—but it's a heck of a way for God to teach me that lesson.

Our lives are filled with lessons. I will tell you mine and hope they resonate with you. And I hope you are inspired by my story, as I have been by the stories of others.

Mine begins with the desperate trauma of my mother's passing. Even decades later, the memory can still make me weep.

CHAPTER 1

Memories of My Mother

My mother died when I was six. I don't have many memories of her, but the ones I do recall are precious. Beyond being a loving, caring mother to me and my older siblings, Nancy and Cecil, she was an admired person in her community.

She graduated as a member of the first nursing school class at the University of Oklahoma in 1959. I still have her yearbook of the graduating class that combined the medical school with the nursing school. Going through that book, I experienced a God Winks moment. Let me explain.

In 1984, one of the attending physicians in my residency was Gene Harrison, who had left private practice to take on the instructional position. He did, however, bring his former practice into the residency clinic, and we saw many patients he had delivered as newborn infants years before. On more than one occasion, I'd be with a patient who would ask, "Is Dr. Harrison here?"

I was almost always able to say yes.

"Could you go get him?"

I always did, and he'd come and inevitably greet his patient with a hug. I called it "The Harrison Hug." Seeing that close relationship with no barriers between doctor and patient touched me so profoundly that I also made hugging part of my own practice. I called it the non-financial bonus of practicing medicine. Hugging someone you haven't seen for a while is emotional and affirming.

I came across my mother's yearbook when my father died in 2017. As I paged through it, past the photos of my mother and the other nurses, there was Dr. Harrison, posing exactly the way I was used to seeing him when I was a resident—feet up on the table, head bowed, and eyes closed. He had been a good napper all his life.

Today, when I think about my mother and nursing school, Dr. Harrison and his hug inevitably come to mind.

My first memory of my mother is her involvement in childhood immunizations. I was four when she went to Stand Watie Elementary School, my public school, to administer vaccinations to children. She was particularly passionate about the polio vaccine, delivered via a few drops on a sugar cube. Her mother, my granny, had contracted polio as a child. Her right leg was about eight inches shorter than her left, and she always had to wear a cumbersome brace on the affected leg.

Granny shows up in a lot of my early memories. When my mother died, Granny was there for us. She was determined we were going to be loved and looked after.

Another memory of my mother: One day, I walked home alone from kindergarten, a distance of about six or eight blocks. It wasn't unusual back then to do that, but on this occasion, my mother wasn't home. She pulled into the driveway just as I was wheeling my bicycle out to our busy street to look for her. My mother leaned out the car window and started laughing. "Where are you going?"

"I was going to find you," I said.

She laughed again and walked me back inside.

One day, my mother piled my sister, Nancy, my brother, Cecil, and I into the car and drove to the Louis Pasteur building near one of the local hospitals. She pulled into the parking lot and left me in the back seat while she took Nancy and Cecil inside. I sat, wondering how long they would be. I suspect it was only twenty minutes, but to this day, I remember the exact parking space my mother had pulled into.

When they came back, Cecil and Nancy were both crying. What had happened in that imposing three-story structure? My mother told me they had both had warts burned off. I made a vow right then and there, "If I ever get a wart, I'm not going to say a word. I'm not going to go through whatever they went through." Years later, when I felt something on my back, I thought, "That feels like a wart. I'm not going to say a word."

In 2022, I experienced another God Winks moment. I had to see a pulmonologist for a follow-up visit to my bout with COVID-19. His office was in the Louis Pasteur building. The parking spot I'd sat in decades before was empty—and I drove right by it, but still, I instantly relived the day when I sat waiting for my mother and siblings to return. Interestingly, the Pasteur building was part of the hospital system I was working for at the time.

My mother was never ill. She was full of life and joy. She was the community nurse, organizing vaccination clinics as well as childbirth classes. I suspect she approached her patients and clients with the same warmth and care she lavished on her family. Oddly, one of my clearer memories is how she made peanut butter. She would take a giant jar of it, upend it all into a bowl, add honey, stir it up, and then scoop it back into the jar. It was a labor of love. And she always cut the crusts off my sandwiches. Cecil and Nancy would tease me, but I stood firm. I would not eat the crust.

My mother was my safe place. She was home, and home was a good and warm place to be. Her warmth also extended beyond our walls. She often took us to visit her parents, who she looked after with great care.

She died on October 8, 1963, only a month after we moved into her dream home. She was not ill. We didn't even know she was going to the hospital that day. My father simply dropped us off at our friend's house, the Cox family. They had twin boys similar to Cecil and my age and two older daughters. One, the youngest, was my sister's best friend. Their father and my dad worked together at Tinker Air Force Base.

We were thrilled at the prospect of playing with our friends all day. They had a pool table and a perfect climbing tree in the backyard. We were having fun right into the evening, and at about eight or nine, somebody said, "Your dad's here."

We ran to the front room that he'd just entered with the preacher, Charlie Dowell. My dad's face was scrunched up, his shoulders stooped, his body trembling. He put a big hand up to his eyes, rubbing vigorously. The preacher looked down at his shoes, then back up at us. Then my father finally said, "Your mother has passed away."

She had been my anchor and my home. Did I imagine a future without her? I don't know. But I was a boy who cared about others, so I suspect I was hurting, maybe not desperately in that moment, but it was a hurt that would grow over the next days and weeks. I believe I blocked out a lot of that early childhood pain. Would it be overwhelming, even today? Perhaps.

It wasn't until much later that I pieced together the full story. My father told us she had pain in her right lower abdominal area. Because she was a nurse and the official "family doctor," she may have decided surgery was the best option. The doctors at the hospital thought it was either her appendix or an ovarian cyst. They completed the surgery, and in my father's words, "They gave her the wrong gas."

When the anesthesiologist walked through the door of the operating room, he went straight to my father and handed him a piece of paper. "This is my fault," he said. "Here's the phone number for my malpractice insurance."

On the morning of the funeral, my father told me I had to wear a suit and tie. I despised wearing suits, even at age six. I ran around the house in a bid to escape, even hiding in a tiny closet. My father and Granny finally wrestled me into the suit and tie. The small Presbyterian church was packed so full they had to pull out extra chairs. All my mother's friends and neighbors were there, as well as her colleagues from the hospital and nursing school. I'm betting the anesthesiologist was there too. I heard he took his life years later after descending into a pit of alcohol and drug abuse and, probably, a deep depression. The anesthesiologist and my mother were very good friends, having gone through school together and worked with one another.

I don't know what the preacher said, but after the service, when he asked my dad if we wanted to view the body, my father said, "No."

It took a lot of years for me to understand the importance of closure. At the time, I was just a little boy missing his mother.

After the funeral, I went back to school. I felt it was important to tell my teacher why I had been absent. I explained that my mother had died. She said, "I know." It felt to me like she was brushing me off. But of course, news travels, especially among teachers. She may have thought she was sparing me the pain of retelling a story that still felt raw.

My birthday was October 17, a week after my mother's death, and the neighborhood kids told me I wasn't going to have a birthday because I no longer had a mother. I ran to my granny, crying. Why couldn't I have a birthday anymore?

She hugged me and left, telling me much later she'd had to go home because her heart was breaking for me. But she didn't leave it at that. She'd promised herself she'd be the strong one for us, so she told my grandfather what the kids had said, and between them, they put on the best birthday they could possibly create.

My grandfather borrowed a pony and had a pony cart built. To the surprise and delight of the neighborhood kids, we had pony and pony cart rides. I'm sure we had a cake and candles, but the pony was the star that day and overshadowed everything else. I could have a birthday even if I didn't have a mother.

In my heart, I always had a mother. On October 19, 2015, I received an award, "Friend of Nursing," from the Oklahoma Nursing Association. On my way home, I made a stop by my mother's gravesite to share it with the person most responsible for leading me to that recognition.

CHAPTER 2

My Stepmother and Lessons Learned

After my mother died, my granny did everything she could to make sure we felt loved and had a stable home. I think my father genuinely loved her. She was a strong link to his wife, who he never forgot—not for one minute of the day.

My father hired housekeepers to look after us while he worked. They lived in a spare room and we got pretty close to some of them. One, who had a daughter my age, was with us for a couple of years. We also had an older woman for a time. They took pretty good care of us, but they weren't mom.

My granny encouraged my father to socialize. He was lonely and missed my mother terribly. He started attending a "Parents without Partners" group in a local church basement and went out on a couple of dates but never brought anybody home to meet us—until Peggy. They had a small wedding on October 9, 1967, and I remember my father telling us to give Peggy a hug. We thought about it and decided not to, or maybe we just forgot. I didn't resent her—I don't think any of us did, but we just weren't that close to her yet. I was actually excited about having a stepmother because it meant we were going to be a family again.

I was also excited about having a younger sister. Baby Angela was born in April 1968, and of course, that changed the family dynamic. Peggy didn't coddle us. We learned to be independent and to look after ourselves, and that included doing our own laundry when we were teens, even if we had to take it to the laundromat because Angela's baby clothes were in the machine for days, just waiting to get done.

Peggy was never unkind to us, but she never showed us the affection she showered on her own daughter. And that was understandable. She did her best, always cooking us a good meal every night and gathering everyone around the dinner table.

Nancy, Cecil, and I spent a lot of time at our friends' houses, not because we didn't like Peggy, but because of the frequent tension between her and my father, usually due to disagreements about us kids.

As a child, those conflicts were often frightening. As an adult, I understand their cause and even empathize with how my stepmother must have felt, knowing my father still loved our mother more than he could ever love her. They also argued over my granny, who my father defended vigorously, probably because she was one of the strongest connections to his dead wife.

Peggy got mad at us, too, sometimes, and I wonder today if it was spill-over from frustration with my dad. When she became angry, frustrated, or moody, we withdrew. We rarely knew or could predict what would set her off. My father would take us all to visit my granny, including Angela when she was a baby. Our granny always wanted her and treated her as another much-loved grandchild. But, as Angela grew up, she may have realized that Peggy took second place to my mother in my father's heart, and that may have started a circle of resentment and a sense of separation from us. Truthfully, my father and stepmother would likely have divorced, but divorce wasn't as common back then. Peggy and Dad were both committed to family, each in their own way.

Every family is dysfunctional in its own unique fashion. I am sure there were times Peggy resented having to raise us, and honestly, we didn't make it easy, especially not when we were teenagers. I wonder if she would have felt less bitter if my father had genuinely loved her. I'm sure the family dynamics would have been vastly different.

Our home situation continued to be enough of a struggle over the years that when my brother and I came home from college in the summer, we'd rent an apartment to maintain independence and improve harmony. We stayed at the house over the Christmas and Thanksgiving holidays, and it got easier when we were adults. To be fair, Peggy always welcomed us, and I suspect her issue was with my father, not us.

Peggy also had a daughter from a previous marriage who was about fifteen years older than me and living on her own when my father married Peggy, but he was afraid that if he died first, she'd give everything to her daughter. Consequently, he made two wills, the second one mostly additions to the first, handwritten with a ballpoint pen, asking my sister, Nancy, to split everything four ways, which she did. But even when my father was at the end of his life, if we mentioned our mom to him, our words would light up his face. He would become a different person—a man with a soft center full of love for a woman he missed dearly.

Every Memorial Day, Dad, Nancy, Cecil, and I would load up the 1966 Chevy Impala and drive to Mom's grave to lay flowers while Peggy and Angela visited Peggy's family gravesite a hundred yards away in the same cemetery. Memorial Day was always tense in the Drabek household.

When my dad died, we honored his wishes and buried him beside my mother. Peggy is buried in her family plot. Unfortunately, Angela was not comfortable attending Dad's graveside service, and I respect that decision.

Dad loved Angela and was proud of her and supportive of her achievements, frequently talking about her accomplishments. Angela spent quality time with Dad, sharing events and activities they both enjoyed right to the end of his life.

When Peggy was approaching the end of her life, I thanked her for making Nancy, Cecil, and me self-sufficient and independent. I'm glad I had the opportunity to do that and that Angela was there as well. I owe a great deal to Peggy, who had such an influence in making me the person I became during some difficult years in my life. She died June 5, 2000, after a five-year battle with uterine cancer.

This chapter of my life was really about lessons learned and the unusual way we learn them. Nobody will treat children better than their own parents. That became clear to me over a lifetime of seeing children who needed guidance. I tried to help them and realized how challenging it was to take on this most important job of raising and supporting the next generation.

Reflecting on my own childhood, my siblings and I were never without the important things we needed. I understand that I would have led a different life if my mother had not died, but I have had a good life, and I attribute some of that to Peggy. The challenges she experienced in being a parent to us helped make me who

I am, and to quote my favorite musician, Dan Fogelberg, it is all "part of the plan," and the plan often presents difficulties that all work out in the end. I am proud of the me I became. The best lessons in life can often be painful. I am blessed and thankful for what I learned.

CHAPTER 3

The Teen Years

The neighborhood we moved to just before my mother died gifted us kids with great friends. Next door lived three boys, Cecil and my age—Steve and the twins, Mark and Mike. Their bedroom window was ten feet across the fence from ours, making it easy to arrange midnight "sneak-out-and-meet" events. Across the street lived Mike, and a few years later, Rodney and his parents moved into a house just around the corner. It was Rod's house where Cecil and I took respite when things got tense at home.

I liked hanging out with my friends in their homes, but if ever I saw or heard one of them being disrespectful to their mothers, I'd feel a strange discomfort inside and would leave the room. There was a short period of time when they'd refer to their mothers as "woman." I didn't like that one bit. I suspect my heart was too full of love for my mother to be able to bear it. Didn't my friends see what a treasure they had and how lucky they were to be able to call someone mom?

Sometimes, they would jokingly call their moms "Ma," and the mothers understood and even played along. I could never call Peggy that. My mother would have gone along with it, too, but not my stepmother. I had constant reminders of what I had lost. I didn't have a mother I could run to or call if I was upset and in need of reassurance. I didn't have someone I could hug who would hug me back and be reluctant to let me go.

But that was part of growing up. Another part was all the "normal" things we did. One day, my father took me to the local hardware store and bought me a brand-new Schwinn Stingray bicycle. "You can ride it home," he said, and I rode it the half-mile back, pedaling as hard as I could up a steep hill, gasping for air but as proud as if I was on top of the world.

My grandfather taught Cecil and me how things work. He was good with anything mechanical, and we were willing students. One day, he did what he called "grinding the valves" of the lawn mower, and we used that engine to turn my Stingray into a minibike that I rode up and down all the streets of south Oklahoma City, always keeping an eye out for black and white police cars and motorcycles. I never got caught, but if I spotted one, I'd duck up someone's driveway or skitter behind a hedge and across a front yard. Then, we built a go-kart that we also rode on the streets.

My grandfather and grandmother Drabek lived on a farm in Wynnewood, Oklahoma, where we and my dad's brothers and sister, and all the cousins went for

Christmas. I remember that as such a wonderful time. For Thanksgiving, we always rented the Czech Hall for a huge family gathering, eating till we could barely walk. We also had a shelter for the July 4th Family Reunion in Will Rogers Park, again with all the cousins there, running through the park all day long.

Every holiday was an extended family occasion, except Memorial Day when we went to the cemetery to pay respect at Mom's gravesite.

There were glorious times when Cecil and I and my cousin, Claude, would spend a week or two at the farm, ostensibly to help our grandfather with chores. Honestly, until we were older and helped with the haying, I think we created more work than what we contributed, but we had wonderful times. It was on the farm that I was introduced to the joy of fishing. As a result of the passion I developed there, my son, Tyler, and I have been on countless fishing trips to Alaska, Canada, and to local lakes and rivers. One of those trips, in July 2024, was with my daughter, Madison, who out-fished me to both our delight.

Even in college and medical school, my friends and I would visit the farm and camp out for a night or two at one of the ponds that we dubbed Lake Tranquil, nestled inside a large oak forest, so hidden that if you didn't know it was there, you'd never find it.

I grew up in the shadow of my cousin, Claude, who attended a private high school where he seemed to always make good grades. He enjoyed books and read a lot of them. I didn't. My granny was an English teacher and wanted Cecil and me to attend summer school, specifically to study English. What? School in the summer? Not a chance!

Today, I wish I'd taken her up on it.

Everyone assumed Claude was going to be the family doctor, and wasn't that wonderful? Growing up hearing about Claude's achievements was annoying at best. Years later, all my assumptions about Claude were upended when he told me that when I was just a baby, my grandma said I would grow up to be a doctor. When Claude was in college, he told her that he hoped to go to medical school. She said, "Oh no. Steve's going to be the doctor."

Claude's mother was Aunt June, and she was like a second mother to me. She was a princess—a queen—a lifeline. She'd loved my mother and, along with my granny, was determined that Cecil, Nancy, and I would have a normal childhood. She was always there for us. I may not have had a mother to call when I needed advice, help, or comforting, but I had Aunt June, and that was pretty darn good.

I loved singing. We had two television shows we always watched: *Sing Along with Mitch* and *The Lawrence Welk Show*. My love of music skyrocketed later in life when I discovered Dan Fogelberg. His songs got me through a lot of difficult situations, especially when I reflected on my life, with all its God Winks, realizing they were just *"Part of the Plan."*

It took a while for me to get seriously interested in girls, but in high school, a friend was dating Vickie, who I had a crush on from the time I sat next to her in tenth-grade science class. She and my friend, Jack, finally parted ways, opening the door for me to make my move. We started dating and even got engaged during my college years. The engagement only lasted two days because her ex persuaded her to think about it. She gave the ring back and I promptly returned it for a refund. But Vickie and I remained friends. We had lost our mothers about ten days apart, and I think we provided special support for each other through some difficult times. Her mother died in a motor vehicle accident, while mine died due to an anesthetic error. Both our worlds were shattered in similar ways.

My father was thrilled that I wasn't about to get married at age eighteen. He'd been saving money for my education, and when I went to college, he received funding to help pay for it from my mother's social security benefits until I completed my Bachelor's degree. He was never able to say "I'm proud of you" or "I love you" after losing Mom. But he showed affection in other ways, like buying dinner after church on Sundays or by paying for anything I needed—and I needed a fair bit during those years in college and medical school, even though it was a path I took entirely by accident.

CHAPTER 4

College

In the fall semester of my senior year of high school, I had classes for only three hours, allowing me to work half-days at Heath Wheel Alignment, an automotive repair shop, which counted for the credits I received in automotive classes at high school. I remember Orville Looney, my auto mechanics teacher, with respect and fondness. I think he liked me because I had a natural talent for it. Even today, I have a genuine interest in fixing things; I guess I'm somewhat of a "Do-It-Yourself King." I'd come to school for only the first hour, wearing my dark blue, slightly stained mechanics uniform, a name tag sewn over the breast pocket—and feeling darn proud about it, too.

In my final semester, I only had a one-hour class in geometry, meaning I could work more hours, earning enough money to buy a 1967 Camaro Rally Sport for seven hundred and fifty dollars. I did a fair amount of drag racing in that car. I had a motorcycle, too, a Honda 750cc with straight pipes, high-rise handlebars, and a sissy-bar. I was proud of that bike. In fact, I wish I still had both the Camaro and the bike. They were my identity. If someone mentioned my name, the response would invariably be, "Oh yeah—Steve. He's the guy who drives the Camaro and he's got that cool bike."

Bill Heath, the owner of the shop where I worked, treated me like a son. We'd have conversations under the hood of a truck or a '57 Chevy with mile-long fins. "Whatcha gonna do after high school, Steve?"

"I don't know, Bill. I guess I'm just gonna keep working."

When summer arrived, I graduated, and I kept on working.

My older sister, Nancy, had been attending Southwestern Oklahoma State University in Weatherford and needed help moving back there that August. "Steve," she said. "Will you and Cecil help me move back into my apartment in Weatherford?"

Sure, I could take a day off work. I had a Camaro, Cecil had a Nova, and Nancy drove a Malibu. You can't fit much into those vehicles, but we crammed everything we could into the back seats, trunks, and passenger's sides, and Cecil and I drag-raced all the way down the I-40 to Weatherford.

It took us about thirty minutes to move everything into Nancy's apartment, and then she said, "Come on, I'll take you on a tour of the college."

Sure. That sounded like fun. So, we walked around the campus. It was a fine sunny day, and we had to admit, with its big old oaks and maples and wide swaths of lawn, it looked like a fine place. Our last stop was the registrar's office, where we signed up to begin classes a week or two later. No one will ever convince me that Nancy didn't know what she was doing right from the minute she asked us to help her move. Essentially, she tricked us into going to college. Today, she does not remember those events, but I will never forget them.

But I didn't mind. I liked spontaneity, and I just shrugged and said, "What the heck! Let's see where this road leads me."

Cecil was a year older, but we registered and started classes together. When we checked in at our dorm, they assumed we were twins, and Cecil became my roommate. We had shared a small bedroom our entire lives and were both glad to be there together, but not as roommates. The next semester, we parted ways, and he moved down the hall.

My intention was to study industrial arts—welding and mechanical stuff basically. But then, biology sidetracked me. I'd liked the subject in high school, and it was the class where I met Vickie, but best of all, it was being taught by Dr. Henry Kirkland. In our first class, he stood up in front of the room full of anxious freshmen students and said, "Okay, this is biochemistry 101."

Instantly, we panicked. We were freshmen and this was all so very new to us. And then he laughed, which made us laugh too. He made biology so much fun we could hardly wait to get to class. His language was familiar and he used examples from life we could all understand. Years later, he was my inspiration. He'd had a gastrectomy (removal of his stomach) early in his life, but he had adapted and moved on. Years later, his example gave me hope that my life would return to normal after surgery as well.

I liked my welding class. I didn't like English all that much, but I did enjoy the speech class. On the final day of the latter, I fell asleep in the back of class after giving my speech, paying no attention to who was up after me. Apparently, I was also talking in my sleep because, when I woke up, the teacher was saying, "Aw, bless his heart."

In the fall of 1975, during my sophomore year, I decided to enroll at the University of Oklahoma for the simple reason it was a bigger campus, and that meant more girls. Well, I was wrong about that, but Vickie was there, and we were still dating off and on and didn't really break up until I started medical school.

I didn't pull down terrific grades at OU, and I was still working weekends with Bill Heath, telling him I wasn't particularly happy at my new school. At Christmas, he asked, "Steve, what are you going to be doing in the spring?" I decided I'd work for Bill full-time.

On New Year's Eve, 1975, Bill had a massive stroke and died about ten days later. His wife took over the business and I continued working there that spring. The other worker, Ernie Pitts, didn't get along well with Bill's wife and left to work at a Gulf filling station where they had built a shop just for him. Bill's wife told me that summer that her husband had been talking about working me into the business in some fashion. Clearly, God had other plans.

That fall, I headed back to Weatherford, Oklahoma, and Southwestern. This time, I took more biology classes, possibly influenced by my sister, Nancy, who had a medical technology degree, but I also just liked the subject and learning how things worked and why. I made a new set of friends in the dorm that year, almost all of them pre-med and pre-dental. As that group of friends grew, so did my interest in what they were doing until I finally said to myself, "You know, medicine sounds like a cool thing to do."

Still, I didn't shift all my courses to reflect my new interest and probably wasn't fully prepared when I applied to medical school the first time, essentially at the last minute. I had only days left when I discovered my application was incomplete and didn't include my short time at OU. On the Thursday afternoon before the deadline, I drove from Weatherford to the OU campus, a ninety-minute drive, getting there in forty-five minutes. I walked into the registrar's office minutes before closing time, knowing my transcripts would have to be in the mail the next day.

The formal entry process required a pre-med interview. On the board were professor Dr. Cole, who taught physiology, a subject I had not yet taken, and the dean of the pharmacy school, who was rather pompous. It was my first interview ever, and I was nervous—plus I had to wear a suit, which I still despise. I was absolutely not prepared.

I spoke about the importance of knowing patients on an individual and personal level in order to be able to deliver better care. The dean asked for an example. Thoroughly intimidated, I stuttered, threw out a lot of ums and uhs, and basically sucked. I didn't get in.

A year later, after taking Dr. Cole's physiology course, I interviewed again, this time for both the University of Oklahoma and the osteopathic school. The interviewer asked, "Why did you not get in the first time?"

"I'm not sure," I said.

He looked over my papers from the previous year. "Your application letter sucked," he said. "Now, after a year, you're the best candidate." Because he chaired the pre-med committee, Dr. Cole wrote my letter of recommendation, and now he knew me quite well, making an "A" in his physiology class.

Then, I had my second pre-med interview with the same people as the previous year. This second time, I walked in with confidence. At the end, the dean of pharmacy, who still scared everyone, said, "Mr. Drabek, do you have any questions?"

"No sir," I said. "But I would like to answer a question from last year." And I talked about the importance of doctors knowing their patients personally. "If I have a young, healthy patient with a breast lump, I will approach the case differently if I know her grandmother had breast cancer. She needs more support and more reassurance, and she'll only get it because, as her grandmother's physician, I know what she's been through and her fears."

A year previously, I'd been a wallflower. That day, the flower wilted. In medical school, it died.

CHAPTER 5

Medical School

I was waiting for my acceptance letter with some degree of anxiety since this was my second time applying to the University of Oklahoma School of Medicine. The interviews had gone well and I felt good about the second time around. Then, one day, as I was walking down the hallway, a fellow student, whose father was a family doctor in Watonga, Oklahoma, and who sat on the admissions committee, popped her head out of a classroom. "Hey, my dad said you got accepted!"

I gave her a hard stare. "This had better not be a joke."

Two days later, the formal letter came and I let the world know. Pretty quickly after that, all my friends converged on the little thirty-foot rundown rental trailer where I lived to help me celebrate. I had two sets of friends. The first brought a big bottle of Mountain Dew; the second group came that evening, and we toasted my new learning adventure with something a bit stronger.

But that was in the spring, and Medical School didn't start until August. I was determined to make good use of the time to get my life together. First, my brother Cecil and I bought a house together. By now, Cecil was helping manage a small family-owned oil company.

Three years later, Cecil got married and purchased my half of the house. Fortunately, my financial house was in order because the process of obtaining loans for a medical education was streamlined and my parents were there for back-up.

I was pretty excited, and maybe I was naive, expecting medical school to be a grown-up professional place. To my surprise, it wasn't much different from college. If anything, the hi-jinx were more intense and probably more risky and risque.

Our class of about one hundred and ninety was broken up into modules of between twenty and twenty-five each. The module became your medical school family. Mine contained every possible type of personality, from brash to shy and from deeply analytical to wildly spontaneous.

At our orientation for our first two years, which was ninety percent book and classwork, the instructor said, "Let me remind you, most of you here are from colleges where you consistently got A's in all your classes. That will not be the case here."

I sat back, shocked. What did that mean? Did they not want us to do well? Or was this just going to be a lot harder than I'd thought? Yes, it was harder in terms of what we had to learn for each exam, comparable to our undergraduate final exams at the end of the semester. We covered that much material every two weeks, and we had five or six classes for each of the four semesters in the didactic years of medical education.

As it turned out, the students who had graduated from larger universities had better test-taking skills than those of us from small colleges who had more interpersonal interactions with our professors. They were able to analyze and navigate the tricky test questions that I tended to take at face value. I had some catching up to do.

Since modules were set up alphabetically, I developed a close friendship with Scott D. He stood out from day one because, on our first day, he announced, "I'm the smartest Son of a Bitch in this class." I was flabbergasted.

He raised a few eyebrows, hackles, and tempers, but his assessment proved to be accurate. He was consistently top of the class. His persona was hard-hearted, cold, and aloof, but rather than turn away from him, I got curious. It took me about five years to figure out that his hard shell protected a soft inner core. Scott and I became friends, going through our residency together after graduating from med school.

He had brilliant memorizing skills—and we had to remember a lot. We used limericks and mnemonics, often laced with profanity or pornographic images, to remember concepts or parts of the body. The one I recall most clearly is the branches of the external carotid artery in the neck, which a cardiothoracic surgeon asked me about during a surgery. I was never so proud to remember that mnemonic and still do to this day.

Many in our module were outspoken, productive, and smart. I tagged along with them, picking up some of their studying skills. In those early days, I can only describe my state of mind as "intimidated" and, at times, frustrated. It took a while for that to settle down to mere tension and anxiety. Looking back, though, I can see that intimidation was a good motivator for getting to know my outstanding classmates and making lifelong friends.

Those were the days before the Privacy Act and HIPAA issues. So, our instructors posted our grades by our social security numbers, not our names, but still in alphabetical order. Many students managed to memorize certain classmates' social security numbers in order to know who was doing well and who was barely getting by with exams. By the time we entered our second year, the administration got wise to what was going on and made a change to the postings, but the limerick kings kept track of test scores anyway, just not bragging about it quite as much.

Those first two years were tough. We went to class—all of us except a few who preferred to read the textbooks and the NoteGroups from the lectures. NoteGroups were created by an assigned person who took detailed notes of each lecture that they would then type up, print out, and hand around to the entire class. I had that responsibility about four times. The NoteGroups were invaluable to use as a study aid for the tests. They were also a terrific medium for artwork in the margins or occasionally pasting obscene cartoons and adding clever comments that might poke fun at a classmate or start a rumor about them. Maybe it wasn't exactly professional, but definitely entertaining and perfect for blowing off steam and frustrations. NoteGroups were also used to challenge the test answers, and this was performed by the class "Bitch" (male or female), an elected position.

After two years of unrelenting classroom work, we began our clinical rotations in hospitals at the University of Oklahoma Health Sciences Center. Professionalism was very much on display now, at least in the patient areas. Otherwise, shenanigans continued as before. The surgeons were quite rigid most of the time but occasionally laughed at the students' answers to questions that they would dream up. The chief resident once asked me the most outrageous question on urology rotation: "Dr. Drabek, how much does a man's hematocrit drop when he develops an erection?"

I answered, "Minimal."

After the laughter died down, the chief resident said, "Maybe for you, personally."

I smiled.

The clinical rotations associated with surgery of any type left me intimidated again, and though keeping us on our toes was deliberate on the part of the surgeons, the rotations became enjoyable compared to classroom work. I would have liked to have specialized in a surgical discipline because of my mechanical background, but the mind games turned me away. I wouldn't have survived the physical and mental tactics, not to mention five to ten more years before earning an income.

Clinical experiences went by the old adage of see one, do one, teach one. Rotations were physically brutal. We sometimes had to be at the hospital at 4 a.m., often working until 8 p.m. But we learned a lot. As students, we were taught by the residents, who were supervised by the attending physicians.

Once, when I was on a pediatric rotation, one of the residents decided to make me suffer. I had no idea why. Analyzing it years later, I thought it might have been that I got along with everyone, and the patients and nurses seemed to like me more than him. He was determined to make me repeat the rotation. Luckily, the attending physician disagreed with him and I made it through, although the stress took its toll.

Our grading system revealed a good deal of favoritism. If you were on a rotation that wasn't your specific interest, and if your lack of interest became known, they likely wouldn't give you as good a grade. The surgeons always gave better grades to wanna-be surgeons. Once we figured it out, we'd say whatever the rotation we were on was definitely our area of interest, despite there being no way in hell some of us would follow that particular clinical career path. However, I enjoyed all rotations during those two years on clinical courses.

Some residents simply wanted to torment us, and even after we declared our specialty, if we were moving out of Oklahoma City, we got a lower grade. My friend, Scott, at the top of the class, didn't escape the system because when he declared he was going to Tulsa (still part of OU Medical School) and they wanted him to remain in Oklahoma City, he was given a lower grade. He chose Tulsa because it was his future wife's home and she planned to return home as an ICU nurse.

Some people did drop out for various reasons. It was just too tough and sometimes cruel. One of the most difficult rotations was thoracic surgery, involving grueling hours every other night on call with pediatric heart surgery. The attending physician was brilliant, Johns Hopkins trained and known for being tough on all in the name of education. But if he sensed you felt intimidated, he'd make it a point to teach you more intensely and follow up with frequent questions. One of my female classmates, who made excellent grades, chose the field of surgery, not a woman's field at that time. Shortly after surviving thoracic surgery in her internship year, she chose to take her own life with no explanation. She was observed gathering IV fluids and potassium. At home, she started an IV and gave herself a large injection of potassium, resulting in her heart stopping.

While rotating in obstetrics and gynecology with labor and delivery, I met Karen Merriman, a cute, perky, and intriguing nurse. With this rotation, medical students were always told to respect the labor and delivery nurses because if they didn't trust you, they would make your life miserable. But if they liked you, they could be instrumental in helping you learn basic skills and procedures for labor and delivery. They were also known for being fun, but only if they trusted your skills and knowledge.

Karen was one of the best nurses there and is still the best nurse I have ever known. Early on, I noticed she had one interesting physical characteristic. Her nail beds were thickened, almost resembling a condition called "clubbing." In medical school, we had learned that it could be associated with dreadful conditions, including advanced lung disease or emphysema, but there was a particular quote in the literature that struck me in 1983: it could be associated with cancer of the esophagus. I remember thinking, very specifically, "I'm not sure I should be involved with someone that might develop esophageal cancer."

I believe I mentioned earlier that God has a wicked sense of humor.

Regardless, I was taken with Karen, so I tried to get her phone number. Paging through the telephone book, the only Merriman listed in the Oklahoma City area was a man named Doyle.

I was stymied, but without another option, I dialed the number. Happily, it was indeed hers. The next obstacle was timing. She worked from 3 p.m. to 11 p.m., but because social events during medical training revolved around happy hours or late nights at various clubs, I ran into her a number of times when she was out with other labor and delivery staff. Since my OB/GYN rotation was in my third year of medical school, I clearly needed a second rotation the next year, not because I wanted to deliver babies—I just needed more exposure to a certain labor and delivery nurse.

The summer before my fourth year, I worked for my cousin Claude, whose father owned an HVAC company. My broad vocational exposure provided by various summer and after-school jobs helped give me the ability to relate and empathize with many of my future patients.

Perhaps the most significant event in the last year of rotations in Oklahoma City was my deepening relationship with Karen. Every year, March has a designated "Match Day," where you are informed of the program to which you matched and where you will do your internship and residency. I had decided to get out of Oklahoma City. I'd lived there all my life, and it was time for something new. I was on that second labor and delivery rotation when Match Day arrived. Karen and I got a fair amount of harassment when the nurses and doctors found out I was going to Tulsa.

Karen was frequently and repeatedly asked. "Are you moving to Tulsa?"

I got a similar question, "Steve, are you taking anyone to Tulsa with you?"

Did I feel any pressure? You bet I did.

Karen and I were married on March 16, 1985, in Oklahoma City. I was in Tulsa, so Karen displayed her organizational talents by planning the entire wedding. Because she had a "real" job, she happily planned and paid for our Hawaiian honeymoon. Fortunately, I was allowed ten days off. At the time, I was on a VA internal medicine rotation in the Muskogee VA Hospital, a rotation that was quite intense with heavy patient loads. It was unheard of for an intern at the VA hospital to take vacation while on that particular rotation. I managed to get approval because the wedding had been planned for some time.

After the wedding and returning from the honeymoon, Karen moved to Tulsa and our new life began. She went to work in labor and delivery at St. Francis Hospital in Tulsa. I started my final rotation as an intern two months later, working in the neonatal intensive care unit, which happened to be right next door to Labor and Delivery. NICU was known for being intense. It was run by a height-challenged macho-type Italian attending who had short-man syndrome. I was six foot one inch. I swear God was winking so much that He had something stuck in His eye.

CHAPTER 6

Diagnosis

My first rotation as an intern in Tulsa was pediatrics, caring for kids in general, but I also had special duties with children with cystic fibrosis. I learned a great deal, especially that this fit exactly with what I wanted to do—working with all age groups in my chosen career of family medicine.

As a medical student, I'd enjoyed my psychiatry rotation, but I didn't feel it would be as rewarding. I believed my best shot at helping people with depression or situational mental health issues would be by knowing them on a personal level, which meant working through short-term, more easily treated mental health issues as opposed to conditions such as schizophrenia or in-depth psychosis.

I rotated through five hospitals in Family Medicine during my internship and residency, including a VA Hospital in Muskogee and an Indian Health Services Hospital in Claremore, as well as the hospitals in Tulsa proper.

Reflecting back to my days as a medical student prior to residency, I fondly remember Brian Geister, a brilliant young doctor in internal medicine who had just become a resident, supervising medical students. Another student and I were the first team he instructed. He eventually wanted to specialize in oncology and start his own practice in that, as well as hematology. Dr. Geister managed to put the fun back into medical training. His approach was energetic, encouraging, and positive, making learning more enjoyable and, therefore, easier. I wanted to emulate his approach in my residency and eventually in my practice as well.

In July 1985, I started my second year of residency and began teaching the incoming interns. That year of residency was mostly elective rotations, but even the required ones were not nearly as intense as the internship year. This year had more responsibilities with teaching and running the Family Medicine inpatient hospital service, where we provided care for patients admitted from our clinics. Electives such as surgical subspecialties, ICU care, and subspecialties that a person had a special interest in were also on the schedule. Mandatory rotations included pulmonary medicine and cardiology, where we cared for more severely ill hospitalized patients. HIV had appeared in my second year as a medical student. During my residency, we were learning a great deal about the disease—and that learning is ongoing.

In January 1987, Karen and I went skiing with a big group of my friends. Karen had never skied and was appropriately terrified, so we enrolled her in a ski course on a carpeted ski slope device in Tulsa, which may or may not have helped. She survived her first and only skiing adventure fully intact. When we returned from Colorado, I got up early one morning to make rounds at St. Francis. I had a cup of coffee to start my day. I was feeling fine, or so I thought. But I vomited and noticed the presence of a minute amount of bright red blood. My mind immediately flashed back to the time I had tried to qualify for the clinical trials for Zantac since I had had reflux much of my life. The doctor was perplexed when I didn't qualify, telling me the biopsy of my esophagus was not normal.

He'd said, "We don't have any good answers for why you have such bad esophagitis, but you should probably have this looked at in about five years."

It was five years, almost to the day.

And then a God Wink occurred. I called Dr. James Beardon (JB), the gastroenterologist I had just finished doing rotations with, and told him my entire story.

In his gruff, off-the-cuff way, he said, "Oh hell, come on in. We'll look at it." His nurse once explained to me that although he had a reputation for being grumpy, he would get mad at situations, never people. I think that description now fits me as well. People rarely understand that part of me and seem to feel I might be angry with them personally.

JB said I had one of the worst cases of esophagitis he'd ever seen and added, "I have looked in thousands of gullets." He set me up the next day for an upper endoscopy and performed about ten or twelve biopsies at 1cm levels down my esophagus. One of them returned with the diagnosis of dysplasia, meaning if cancer were not present now, it would be in the future. However, I was hopeful we could handle it with treatment and so eliminate it. He prescribed bismuth sulfate, the active ingredient in Pepto-Bismol. I remember picking it up at the St. Francis pharmacy, thinking, "Okay, I'm going to do this. Let's get ahead of it." I was anxious but not frightened.

I took the white powder, mixed it with water to make a paste, and swallowed it. He scoped me again several weeks later and announced it was looking better, except for one little spot at the lowest portion of my esophagus just above the stomach, which he biopsied again.

Karen and I were house shopping in Oklahoma City that weekend, and JB told us, "I'm on call this weekend. When you get back from Oklahoma City, just come to the hospital and page me. I'll meet you there."

We drove back on Sunday and I went directly to the hospital while Karen stayed home to prepare for work that night. I paged JB and he told me to meet him on the eighth floor, where he led me into an empty waiting room, closed the door, and said, "Sit down."

In my upbeat, naive manner, I blurted out immediately, "Did the dysplasia improve?"

He said, "No. It's worse." If I had paid closer attention, I might have been able to read between the lines. He didn't have it in him to tell me I had one of the most feared cancers. I know he was crushed. He was a friend, and the thought of saying the word "cancer" was too much for him.

A few days later, I walked down to the pathologist's office in the basement of Saint Francis because, as a young, inquisitive doctor, I was curious about my microscopic biopsy slides. I introduced myself and said, "Do you think we could look at those dysplasia slides so I can get a feel for how bad it is?"

He said, "No. I don't have time, but it wasn't dysplasia—it was adenocarcinoma."

I froze—not just my body, but my heart and mind. Time stopped. When I caught my breath again, I turned and walked out of his office, up the stairs, and out of the hospital. My only thought was, "I don't want to have esophageal cancer."

At home, I dosed myself with more bismuth. Was I hopeful that this was all wrong? That it would go away?

Maybe.

I told Karen when she got home. We held each other, crying. We had been married two years—not the lifetime we were anticipating or promised. I knew the last thing I should do was review information in my medical textbooks at home, so I quietly slipped out to the medical library to look at recent medical literature. I'd studied my texts enough to know they would offer no hope. However, I failed to consider that Karen was at home with those textbooks. The medical literature spoke of three preferred places for addressing my diagnosis: the Lahey Clinic on the East Coast, Iowa, middle of nowhere, and the Mayo Clinic.

JB called the next day because after I'd seen the pathologist, I suspect he'd called him. The Saint Francis Pathologist had trained at the Mayo Clinic and said there was no better place to get the optimum result, because a surgeon there had pioneered the surgery for this cancer. He gave JB the number and the name: William Spencer Payne, M.D. JB spoke to Dr. Payne before he called me and said, "We're going to get you to the best place. I'll call you as soon as I get the phone number we need for the Mayo Clinic."

I was seeing patients in my clinic on a Thursday afternoon when JB called at 3:30 p.m. "I've got the phone number for Dr. William Spencer Payne. He's expecting your call."

I made the call from Dr. Rod Holloway's office, one of the attending physicians for our residency clinic. Dr. Holloway generously offered to see the remainder of my afternoon patients, allowing me to leave for the day. As I dialed the number, I remember thinking, "Gosh, I'm calling the Mayo Clinic. The next available appointment will be weeks away."

I got through to Dr. Payne, who talked to me for a minute and said, "Let me have my secretary look and see when the next available appointment will be for us to see you. I'll put you on hold and the secretary will be right with you."

I was still filled with dread, anticipating a long wait. After all, it was the Mayo Clinic and this was Dr. Payne, the man who had pioneered the surgery I would probably need.

After about a minute, the secretary came on the line. "Can you be here Monday at 7 a.m.?"

I took a deep breath. "I'll be there." I didn't know how, but I was going to make it happen. I'd hitchhike if I had to.

I went home to find Karen sitting at the kitchen table. "What are you doing at home?" I asked. "Aren't you supposed to be working?"

She'd read my textbooks. "I couldn't bear it anymore," she said. "I had to come home."

For the next thirty minutes, we sat at the table, holding each other and crying. Then we realized—we had only three days to make all the arrangements, including finding someone to look after Muggins, our dog. Luckily, we found a travel agent, and an hour later, our one-way plane tickets were booked. When would we come back? Would I be coming back at all?

The cancer scared me, but I was never afraid I would die. I was in God's hands.

Friday evening, we drove to Oklahoma City to give the news to my family and Karen's parents. On Sunday morning, Pat, a fellow resident, picked us up to take us to the Tulsa Airport. As we carried our luggage to Pat's car, I turned and ran back into the house and jumped on the scales to record my weight. I'd been jogging three miles a day for the past few months, trying to get myself into the best possible shape. The scales tipped at 220 pounds. Down ten. I was probably in the best physical condition of my life.

The flight was surreal. I remember thinking about how lucky I was to be going to the Mayo Clinic. At the same time, I still felt absolutely horrified about my diagnosis. I had never before contemplated my mortality. Meanwhile, Karen was thinking about having my child, whether I did well at the Mayo Clinic or not.

Flying into Rochester, we stared in wonder at the fields of crops surrounding what looked like a remote small community. We collected our bags and hailed a cab for the drive to the Kahler Hotel. In all that vast space we drove through, one tall golden building stood out. "What is that tall building in the distance?" I asked the cab driver.

The "Clinic," he said.

In that part of the world, it was simply known as "The Clinic."

We checked into the Kahler Hotel, where the Mayo Clinic had booked a room for us. The hotel was across the street from the hospital and connected to it by tunnels. Karen would have to spend a good deal of time in our tiny room equipped with a water closet. Luckily, her friend, Christy, lived nearby in a small town in Wisconsin and planned to stay with her while I was in surgery.

At 7 a.m. on Monday, April 27, I presented myself at the Mayo Clinic. By now, terror had just about taken over my mind and body. A gastroenterologist gave me a complete physical before Dr. Payne came into the room with his entourage: a doctor from Australia, one from India, two residents, and a fellow in thoracic surgery. I learned later that Dr. Payne was seventy-five, but he still walked tall, carrying himself with confidence and dignity, with eyes that were warm with empathy. I immediately felt comfortable after he explained the surgery.

He said he had reviewed the biopsy from JB and explained how this disease is surgically staged and that CT scans or radiographic studies were not needed. Because I'd had no previous surgery on my belly, he said he could accomplish a total trans-hiatal esophagogastrectomy more easily. The plan was to pull my esophagus up along with my stomach to just behind my heart and out through my left neck area. Then they would excise the esophagus and lesser curvature of the stomach. Finally, they would suture the stub of an esophagus back to what remained of my stomach. Most importantly, they would not cut my chest open. If I wasn't scared before, I was now. But I trusted him. That was the surgery he had pioneered. There was no one better, also, he had trained the physicians at Lahey Clinic and in Iowa doing the same procedure.

Seeing my apprehension and fear, Dr. Payne said, "Dr. Drabek, God has taken care of you for thirty years; why would he stop now?"

Before he turned to leave with his posse behind him, he said, "You're all set. We'll put you in the hospital tonight, do a bowel prep, and operate Tuesday morning."

I wanted to say something, but I was paralyzed with fear. I just said, "Okay."

My next stop was admitting, across the street, at Methodist Hospital. We were escorted to a hospital room and I was given a scheduled bowel prep called Golytely. The term Golytely is a perfect oxymoron. The product's job is to clean out the colon in the event the colon is needed to replace part of my esophagus instead of the tube they created with my stomach. I had to drink a full liter of the Golytely, which makes a rapid transit from the stomach through to the colon, cleaning out undesirable bacteria along with any substances left behind. None of that occurs lightly. I've seen many delicate elderly people drink it without complaint, but this thirty-year-old, healthy-as-a-horse doctor couldn't even finish the entire bottle. Thankfully, I downed enough to serve the purpose. It was my first deep lesson in empathy.

It was also my first experience as a patient. At 5:30 a.m. the following morning, April 28 (now known as my un-birthday), the Foley catheter team came in and placed a catheter. I had bladder spasms until 10:00 a.m., when they wheeled me into the operating room. Fortunately, Karen had Christy, her friend, fellow nurse, and maid of honor with her for the entire six to seven hours. As they wheeled me out of surgery, I remember seeing them on the way to the Intensive Care Unit.

CHAPTER 7

Recovery

Karen leaned down over me to plant a kiss on my forehead. After that, I remember waking up in the ICU the following morning, and one of the first things I heard was a nurse saying, "We'll have you up and walking later today."

I had a chest tube with drainage bottles on each side, my Foley catheter with reservoir, a nasogastric tube, two IV lines, and an arterial line, along with a drain by the left neck area adjacent to the surgery site. I probably also had an epidural catheter for pain. How was I going to walk? The answer was a walker with wheels. I managed three laps around the ICU. Three days earlier, I'd jogged three miles. Come on, God, you're cracking me up!

The ICU nurse took great care of me, even giving me a bed bath. I followed her orders because I was married to a nurse and knew the respect they deserved. Thirty minutes after my bath, the second-year surgery resident on Dr. Payne's team came and explained the procedure he had helped with, most likely by holding a retractor. But if I'd been in his place working with Dr. Payne, I'm guessing I would have been proud, too.

His important piece of news was, "The pathology looks great: a one-centimeter diameter lesion the thickness of a dime, no lymph nodes positive, and no spread beyond serosa." In other words, I was most likely cured through surgery. The medical jargon is T1N0M0; T indicating the size (1cm), N meaning no positive lymph nodes, and M denoting no metastasis, meaning no spread.

Good news! But I said, "I'm sorry. It's not that I don't believe you, but I'll have to see the results in black and white—the written pathology report!"

Given I had just heard a miraculous result of a tedious surgery, and pathology reports back home usually took two to three days before being dictated, typed, and placed in the chart, I probably sounded cold and ungrateful. To my relief and joy, the resident understood and handed me the chart. "Here you go, everything at the clinic is done by frozen section, returned the following morning."

Seeing the report and noting it said exactly what the resident had said, I let myself fully rejoice. No words can adequately describe my happiness in that moment.

Dr. Payne and his team had taken out eighty-five percent of my esophagus along with the lesser curvature and one-third of my stomach due to a dime-sized lesion of a usually devastating cancer. At age thirty, I was essentially cured, thanks to early detection.

The great doctor himself visited later each day, operating on patients first. One day, while I was resting and relaxing to music, Dr. Payne, out on the medical floor, had to tweak my toe to get my attention. I'd brought a Sony Walkman with me, loaded with Dan Fogelberg music. And there I was, eyes closed, doing my best to harmonize with my favorite singer and trying not to feel too sad that my hoarseness meant this particular talent had at least temporarily deserted me.

They had moved me out of the Intensive Care Unit that first day after surgery to the sixth floor of Rochester Methodist Hospital. The following Monday, I was scheduled for a Gastrografin swallowing study to ascertain that the sutures creating the new union of my remaining short esophagus were stable, still joined to my stomach, and not leaking into surrounding tissues. In simple terms, I was swallowing a dye, which went down through a very short esophagus and into my chest, where my relocated stomach functioned more like a conduit, then into my abdomen, where my intestinal contents remained in a somewhat normal position. Finally, the dye filtered down into my colon, exiting normally.

I had decided, even before starting the test, that I would not leave the radiology suite without the resident sharing the results with me. He did and I felt like a little kid on Christmas morning because I got to take something by mouth, even though Gastrografin tasted bad. There were no leaks at the anastomosis, so no contrast dye going into the subcutaneous tissue. Honestly, I was on top of the world. All my prayers had been answered.

Returning to my room, knowing there were no leaks, I realized my nasogastric tube would come out later that day, but probably not until Dr. Payne's entourage arrived, which was going to be quite a bit later in the afternoon. All of a sudden, after having that tube in for days, it now became unbearable. With each swallowing reflex motion, the tube moved ever so slightly, and by now, my throat was raw and sore. I began retching and gagging, totally psyched to get rid of it but knowing it would not be immediately removed. I finally just closed my eyes, took some deep breaths, and reminded myself it had been there a long time and did not bother me until now.

Finally, word came down that Dr. Payne and the residents would soon arrive, and they did, marching down the hall like the American army to see the surgical prisoners. Dr. Payne entered my room, looked around, and asked, "Has anyone seen the results of the swallow study?" I'm sure he was notified of the results personally, but his team stood there, their faces blank. Really? I spoke into the silence, quoting the radiology report given verbally to me early that morning: "Gastroesophageal anastomosis intact with no indication of leakage into surrounding tissue."

Dr. Payne smiled. The report meant mission accomplished. He was a confident man, demonstrating a lesson to those he taught and trained well. Exchanging gratified looks, the team prepared to leave the room. I interrupted, pointing at the nasogastric tube and raising my eyebrows. Then, I began peeling the tape from my nose. Smiling broadly, they left, except for Dr. Marc Schumacher, a reserved, aspiring thoracic surgeon and senior resident on the team, who stayed behind to remove the NG tube before I pulled it myself. I gave him my heartfelt thanks.

And so, I was one step closer to living a "normal" life. Throughout most of that post-operative time, I had a PCA (patient-controlled analgesia) pump to relieve pain, but it also helped me get some sleep in the noisy hospital. The PCA also became quite useful when the team showed up for a procedure or removed a medical intervention previously placed that might result in discomfort or pain—for me. For instance, I definitely hit the button when they came to pull out the big chest tubes that were inserted under anesthesia. After that final procedure of removing the NG tube, my pain pump disappeared. It was replaced with liquid Darvon, the weakest pain med that tasted really bitter but was effective, to my delight.

Ecstatic, I was now finally able to eat. First, I had clear liquids and broth. The first taste of broth was wonderful; the second, not so much. Thicker liquids brought on dumping syndrome and nausea, a condition I still suffer from to this day, although not as frequently.

Dumping syndrome occurs when food, especially rich food, enters the stomach and "dumps" it into the intestine too quickly, leading to cold sweats, shakiness, and, in my case, a pulse rate of exactly 118. Blood sugar often drops and can also draw fluids out of blood vessels into the GI tract, accompanied by a general feeling of nausea. The first time it happened, my anxiety level shot up. The nurse was also concerned and called Dr. Schumacher urgently. When he saw my clammy face literally dripping with perspiration and my mouth gasping for air, he was worried I might be having a pulmonary embolism, which was not uncommon after major surgery. It can often lead to death. Fortunately, that wasn't the issue. But, unfortunately, dumping syndrome became my common unwanted visitor brought on by eating just about anything, especially during those first two years after surgery.

Still, all I had to do was remind myself that I was alive, and that settled me down pretty fast. The rest of that week passed uneventfully. Karen and I spent a lot of time on the eighth-floor outdoor patio, and oh, how wonderful it was to breathe fresh May air and gaze up at a blue sky. I learned so much from being a patient during those two weeks, lessons that had a deep impact on how I practiced medicine for the next forty years.

I was discharged on the morning of Mother's Day, Sunday, May 10. Dr. Doug Green, a resident and friend from Oklahoma who was in training at the Clinic, offered to drive us to the Rochester Airport. Walking to the gate, even in such a small airport, was challenging as I rediscovered muscles I hadn't used for weeks.

Arriving in Tulsa, we realized we hadn't considered how we'd get home. Then I remembered that my good friend, Scott D, the smartest son of a bitch in medical school, lived near the airport. One quick phone call and he was on his way. Waiting for him to arrive, I had time to reflect on Dr. Payne's wisdom and skill. How could I have been so fortunate in so many ways? Perhaps a God Wink?

CHAPTER 8

Practice

Arriving home on Mother's Day was a beautiful piece of serendipity (or a God Wink?) To Karen's mom, I was the son she never had, and seeing her was a blessing.

Dr. Payne had given me strict instructions not to drive for six weeks. Let's just say that I didn't get behind the wheel during rush hour. And then I still had ten weeks left in my residency. I finished up with a lot of empathy and kindness from everyone at the residency clinic. If I needed to rest or lie down, I was told, "Don't worry about it."

Of course, JB assailed me as soon as I got back, demanding I lift my shirt so he could see the scar or, as he said, "What the hell they did." To our great surprise, while we were away, the wives of my fellow residents had gotten together, raising enough money to pay for Karen's hotel bill. The kindness we received was genuine and from the heart. We were beyond grateful and tearfully overwhelmed with their kindness.

All this time, I should have been involved in helping to set up my new practice in Yukon, Oklahoma that I was to share with my colleague, Dr. Chapman. Out of necessity, I'd delegated all the work to him, and he stepped in without a second thought.

I continued to attend educational seminars at the hospital. One day, one of the Internal Medicine residents stopped me as I was walking down the hall. "Drabek! What's up? You look like someone who's got cancer!"

I said, "Well, I did. They took it out."

I finally saw an actual example of the expression "taken aback" when he took a full step backward. Everyone I met in those days had one of two reactions: horrified or amazed.

One of the first things I did when I got home was step on the scale again. During my two-week stay at the clinic, they'd weighed me every morning, as I dropped about 2.2 pounds daily. At one point, I had a flashback to a daydream I'd had when I was eight, where I imagined getting sick, being in the hospital, and losing weight. And so I was actually living my childhood dream, which unfortunately more closely resembled a nightmare. At my last weigh-in at home, I had been 220. I was now down to 192. I wasn't about to gain weight quickly because almost every time I ate, I still became clammy and sweaty, and my pulse rate would rise to 118, indicating what was coming: dumping syndrome. During the operation, they removed my entire vagus nerve, which impacts the heart rate along with intestinal transit activity with cramping and then explosive diarrhea. The feeling was pure misery. I'd be overwhelmed by nausea, but the operation had rendered me unable to vomit. If I was in public on those occasions, people were generally convinced I was having a heart attack. I would absolutely look as bad as I was feeling.

During these episodes, I would frequently turn to Karen and say, "I don't know if I've ever told you this, but I hate nausea."

I think I've spoken those words at least a thousand times.

And then, Karen started having "sympathy nausea." I'd have a small McDonald's hamburger, timing the ride from Tulsa to her parents' house in Oklahoma City, knowing we could arrive in time for me to handle the effects—nausea and diarrhea. Karen wasn't experiencing diarrhea, but her episodes of nausea were becoming more frequent. Then, one night, she said, "My boobs hurt."

Oh.

While I'd been recovering from surgery at the Methodist Hospital, one day, she'd come to my hospital bedside and said, "Well, I guess I am not pregnant." Her menstrual cycle had begun, and because I'd received two or three units of blood during surgery, she wanted to donate blood. I looked at her and said, "Karen, you don't need to worry about that at this point."

Understandably, her nausea had not sent up any warning flags, even if she was a labor and delivery nurse.

But now...

"You could be pregnant," I said.

"How could I be?" she said. "I had a cycle while we were at the Mayo Clinic."

"Give me a urine specimen," I said. "I'll take it to the clinic tomorrow and do a pregnancy test."

The next morning, I asked the lab technician to run the test and not to tell anyone. She did, and later that day, handed me a small piece of paper. On it was written one word: "positive."

Inside, I was jumping with excitement. On the outside, I smiled, "I guess I'd better go run an errand."

I drove to St. Francis Hospital mid-morning and walked to the Labor and Delivery Department. I hadn't been back since my operation, so I was swarmed by nurses and doctors. "How are you doing? You look great! Welcome back!"

Karen came out to the hallway to see what the fuss and activity were about. She had a good idea why I was there. "Well," she said. "It's negative, isn't it?"

I just held up the piece of paper in front of her and her coworkers. The blood drained from her face. And then we were embracing, and while everyone else cheered, she sat down, afraid she was going to faint.

We were doing an internal jig while God winked at us. Months later, in January 1988, we had a beautiful baby girl we named Madison. Then, in another God Wink moment, almost exactly two years later, I once again informed my wife of another pregnancy one evening in my own office this time. In mid-November 1990, we had a baby boy named Tyler by C-section because he insisted on entering the world butt first.

When my colleagues and I completed our stint at the residency program, we had a final ceremony, which was mostly about showing gratitude to our spouses for putting up with us—and rightfully so. No one deserved thanks more than Karen. I suspect she went through more than any of the other wives.

We'd already found a home in Yukon. My new employer, Baptist Medical Center, generously paid for the moving company, who came and efficiently packed up our entire house in one day. Dr. Chapman and I were part of the hospital's outreach that was just beginning at that time, emphasizing primary care involvement in healthcare. Our clinic was on a busy corner next to a strip mall and was due to open on September 6, giving me time after our move on July 2 to become acquainted with some important members of my new community.

Getting to know Yukon was one God Wink after another. My father's childhood home was only miles away, and I quickly became acquainted with Drabeks on the other side of the family, not even knowing there was another side at the time. My grandfather had been an alcoholic. His drinking was a problem for the Drabek family garage business, so he was ostracized to a certain extent. That branch of the Drabeks moved to Wynnewood, Oklahoma to a small farm where my father spent his teen years until going off to war. I found long-lost relatives, some of whom became patients, and learned much more about my family history. The family, in turn, learned about me.

One of the things I especially enjoyed was watching our office building almost literally rising from the ground. I'd go out to the site and walk around it while the dry-wallers were smearing their goo over the cracks and the flooring people were on their knees laying tiles.

Just before we opened our practice, the hospital administrators called to tell Dr. Chapman and me that we should interview a couple of nurses they thought would be a good fit for us. We said, "Great. Set the time and we'll be there."

We hired both nurses. Mine was RaeAnn, an RN who was a pistol: boisterous, extroverted, smart, warm, and fun. I was sold on her in no time flat, but before I could make her an offer, she said, "I'd love to work for you, but just get one thing straight—I don't do vomit."

I appreciated her straightforward attitude, but the fact was, I didn't do vomit either, in more than one sense of the word. First, I never did like it, and second, I couldn't vomit anymore —painful retching was the full extent of my capabilities in that department. But since the operation, I'd begun to better tolerate vomit in general.

RaeAnn was a blessing to the beginning of my new world. The patients loved her and we're still friends to this day.

Another blessing (and a God Wink?) was having Dr. Brian Geister open his oncology and hematology practice in Oklahoma City, only thirteen miles away. I welcomed him with great delight. "Good to see you. I'm glad you're going to be here if I ever need you for my patients, but I hope to never need you personally since my esophageal cancer was hopefully cured with my surgery just a few months earlier."

In 2010, God displayed his wicked sense of humor once again when he confirmed my Chronic Lymphocytic Leukemia. I was convinced the leukemia was at least partially a result of follow-up X-rays and CT scans done every six months for the first two years after Dr. Payne removed my esophagus. Dr. Geister seemed to minimize that consideration, and that was okay because pinning down a cause wasn't about to change anything.

He's my physician, so I do what he tells me to, no matter how begrudgingly, but also with a smile and a laugh. We even went to Mexico together on medical mission trips on four different occasions until drug cartels and crime issues made it too dangerous.

Brian's attitude was and still is upbeat, encouraging, and positive. He is truly a blessing to me and, I suspect, to every patient he has worked with. I trusted him implicitly then, and I still do today.

Baptist Hospital introduced me to the local pharmacists and many business people in the area. Because Dr. Chapman didn't live in the community, I had the great advantage of fitting in much more quickly. My cousin Claude's father owned a business in OKC that was established the year I was born. I had a private, unlisted back line at the office, and one day, my nurse called through to me, "Hey, Drabek. You got someone calling on your private back line. I don't know who it is, but you've got to come talk to them."

I wasn't about to say no to Nurse RaeAnn, so I picked up. The caller was Roy Cook, an 85-year-old gentleman who had worked for the phone company and knew enough people to get my private back office number. We became very good friends, especially after he told me the story of buying eggs from the Drabeks when he worked at the West Side grocery store, pointing out that he'd never felt the need to candle the Drabek family's eggs.

At the time, the medical community was caught up in the new issue of cholesterol, and Baptist Hospital, in its wisdom, offered free cholesterol screening to anyone in the community of thirty-five thousand people. Shortly after our clinic opened, people lined up at our door, down the street, and right into the strip mall parking lot. We were doing so many tests we barely had time to look after our patients.

Meanwhile, we were busy assigning patients who were making appointments to see us. With two new doctors, we figured the best way to handle the issue was to alternate which of us the patient would see. However, some patients had preferences.

One day, my nurse said to me, "Dr. Drabek, there's a lady on the phone who wants to talk to you."

"What about?"

"I don't know. She just asked for you."

Again, never argue with RaeAnn.

I picked up the receiver and introduced myself. She told me her name was Olga, asked a few standard questions, and then said, "I have to ask, does either one of you have a beard?"

I said, "Well, ma'am, I'm the one with the beard, but it's clean. I wash it every day."

"I'm sorry," she replied. "I'll have to see the one that doesn't have the beard."

"That's okay," I said. "Dr. Chapman is a good guy."

About a month later, the woman's niece, who was a physician's assistant, brought her in from her retirement home to see me. First, the niece asked me privately, "Do you remember the lady who asked you about the beard?"

I nodded. "I do."

"You're about to see her. She's my aunt and can be a bit cantankerous at times, but she's a good person."

I walked into the room, introduced myself, and said, "Good morning, Ms. Olga. I understand you don't like people with beards."

She let out a roar of laughter—and that cemented a relationship I treasured until she passed about ten years later, still under my care.

CHAPTER 9

The Practice Grows

D r. Randall Chapman and I had very different approaches to managing our patients. I would describe his as paternalistic, while mine was probably more maternalistic. I created deep relationships with my patients, and I believe I probably built a genuine empathy for them because I'd been a patient myself.

Randall was a good man and an excellent doctor. We both had our own personality quirks, but we got along, especially after we went on a fishing trip to Lake Tranquill on my grandfather's property.

Dr. Chapman and I saw our practice grow. Roy Cook, the retired phone company employee, dropped by regularly, if for no other reason than to give everyone a hug. And that was great until one day, he came in after visiting his wife in her nursing home, where there was an outbreak of scabies.

We were all itchy for a while, and it took us a bit of time to figure out why we were scratching so much and where these darn little mites had come from. When we finally put it all together, we just laughed because we loved Roy and Darlene Cook and couldn't imagine blaming them for anything—certainly not for a few old scabies.

As I settled into my practice, I enjoyed it more and more. It fit with everything I'd wanted to do as a family doctor—building relationships with people and treating the whole person, not just physical symptoms and diseases. Unfortunately, Dr. Chapman discovered he was better suited to emergency care and left the practice after two years to go back to the hospital emergency room. Randall simply didn't have the desire to follow patients longitudinally in their treatment and progress, but I absolutely loved it.

However, there was one case where he did follow a special patient very closely, and I'm glad it was him and not me. While we alternated taking new patients, we also consulted with each other, especially about the challenging or difficult ones. I'm pretty sure it was a God Wink that he was the one assigned to a particularly memorable, fascinating, but emotionally difficult patient whose name, I believe, was Larry. He was a Marine Corps veteran, fifty-nine, and having trouble swallowing. Tests eventually revealed he had esophageal cancer that reflected the textbook description Karen had read. Larry was definitely far advanced upon his initial presentation, and apparently, he was well aware he'd been handed a death sentence. Randall told me his patient had not handled the diagnosis well, and that became clearer as time passed.

One day, Randall came to my office wearing his coat, obviously on his way out the door.

"Where are you going?" I asked.

"Out. I've got to go see Larry."

"Is he doing poorly?" I asked.

Randall let out the smallest sigh. "Yeah. He put a .45 in his mouth—while I was on the phone with his wife, discussing her concern about him. I heard the shot."

I felt a shiver run right through my body.

Dr. Chapman told me the rest of the story later. He went to Larry's house, where he found that his patient had hauled a large four-by-eight sheet of plywood up to the attic, positioned himself in front of it, put the gun in his mouth, and pulled the trigger. He'd hoped to save his family some of the horrific and emotional cleanup from the splattered mess he knew he would make. Randall said the scene was still "god-awful."

I don't know how I would have felt or what I would have done had Larry been my patient. I would have gone to his house, just as Dr. Chapman did, but what would the impact have been? Even hearing the story brought a sense of loss. I was so lucky. I could so easily have been in Larry's shoes, with a diagnosis that would have given me no hope. What a horrific thought!

I never lost sight of my luck or how precarious my situation could be. The first two years after my operation, per Dr. Payne's orders, I had a CT scan every six months, which is why I wonder today if the radiation from so many CT scans and X-rays could have played a role in my Chronic Lymphocytic Leukemia (CLL). But as Dan Fogelberg's song tells the tale, it's "Part of the Plan," or a speed bump in the road of life.

Karen very firmly told me right from the start that she didn't want to know when I was going in for one of my scans—she was interested only in the results. And I understood that—why put her through those hours or possibly days of worry? Dr. Payne had told me at discharge: "The CT scans need to be done because we want to know if the cancer returns."

Thinking back on that, I am not sure I would still accept that as a logical explanation.

My first CT scan at the Baptist Hospital was probably the most interesting. I met the radiologist Dr. Gary Roberts, who became my friend over the years. I told Gary right up front that I was not about to leave the radiology suite until I knew the results. He was fine with that. "I normally don't talk to patients," he said. "I wouldn't be good at that interaction. But this is different."

After the scan, I stood behind him while he read the films. He explained there was a small nodule, probably a small piece of the esophagus where it had been sutured to the stomach, but this unusual piece of tissue, less than the size of a pea, stuck out like a thumb. "We really don't know what this is," he said. "But we can't rule out a metastatic disease."

And that, of course, was why he didn't talk to patients. If I hadn't known what I did, I would have been worried. But I wasn't, even though the radiology report stated it every time I had a scan for the next two years. Dr. Don Murray, my gastroenterologist, noticed it, too. After the last one, the report motivated Dr. Murray to biopsy the tiny piece of tissue that was barely out of my oral cavity. It was benign, and I wasn't surprised. Dr. Payne had described putting together the esophagus, a small round tube, and reconnecting it to the stomach through an incision in my left neck, which left the stomach more like a blob. A thin piece of tissue out of place and protruding inward didn't surprise me one bit.

The biopsy itself had to have been quite a feat, but Don Murray had incredible skills along with a phenomenal bedside manner, only rolling his eyes when he thought I was not looking. Usually, when you biopsy with a scope, it goes down into the patient's stomach.

My stomach was right up close, just below my throat—a challenging endeavor because the scope is still four feet long.

My appreciation for being alive was perhaps one of the factors that led me to my next and possibly greatest medical calling.

CHAPTER 10

The Beginning of Hospice Work

O ne morning in 1990, I was reading the daily Oklahoma newspaper, as I did every day, when I spotted an article about hospice. It caught my eye because of an experience I'd had as a third-year medical student that had a lasting impact on me.

In 1983, I was on my internal medicine rotation at the VA Hospital as a member of the fifth-floor Brown Rotating internal medicine team that we referred to as the "Brown-rot," meaning we had patients on a number of different floors while the other teams had just one floor. Another student and I were on call one night with our supervising internal medicine resident when we admitted Mr. Vanderfield, a veteran in his late eighties, with stage IV small-cell lung cancer. His wife was always by his side. Prior to his most recent diagnosis, he'd had cancer of the larynx, which was surgically removed, so he was non-verbal. His wife was his voice. It was clear he was going to die, but at the time, we had no hospice in Oklahoma City.

It was my honor to take care of him. Every time I entered his room, I'd sit down and have long conversations with his wife, listening to her and looking at him, and always, he had an incredible smile that reached beyond his mouth to his eyes, lighting up his entire face. He communicated through that smile—the smile of an angel on earth. Whenever I had time, I would stop by and visit this mountain of a man and his wife.

He was there for about a week. On one rare occasion when his wife was not by his side, I entered his room to draw blood for lab tests. No one had previously been able to do it. I carefully looked for a vein and said, "Sorry," because I didn't hit it. I didn't hit it the second time, either.

"I'm so sorry!"

He just smiled that incredible smile of his. His lips spelled out, "That's okay. You have to do what you have to do."

I finally hit the vein on the third try. We were now able to monitor parameters, but it made no difference to his final outcome.

One night I was on call, taking admissions and seeing to whatever needed to be done. I was walking down the hall at some late or possibly early morning hour when I passed his room. As always, I looked in. His wife looked up and waved at me. "Steve!"

I walked into the room. She looked up at me, her eyes big. "Is he?"

"I took my stethoscope out of my pocket, plugged it into my ears, and placed it on his chest to listen for his heartbeats. His final expiration came just as I began.

I heard no heart tones after the release of his last breath.

Tears spilled over my eyes.

His incredible smile left him only when he died. However, I was consoled, knowing he was finally at peace. His wife had maintained her vigil. No panic. No drama. It was the first time I was honored to be involved with an event as emotional as birth, and it created in me a passion for caring for dying people. This was also when I began to part ways with my formal training, which had taught me that death was the worst aspect of caring for people.

I was certain I was called to work with hospice because I believed it was what medicine is about: reducing physical, emotional, and spiritual pain and suffering. Of course, I also never had closure with my mother, and I believe that, too, drew me to hospice— perhaps closure with other humans was a way of achieving it with her.

I wrote an article, *The Incredible Smile*, about my experience with this wonderful patient. I was proud and honored to have it published in the Oklahoma State Medical Association monthly journal. After publication, I received a personal note from Dr. Jesus Medina, the outstanding head of the ENT department. I was suitably wowed.

When I happened upon the article in the Daily Oklahoman newspaper, stating that a hospice was about to be introduced into our community, I saw it as an opportunity. God certainly meant business with that wink. There had been one in the past, but a lack of support had shut it down. At the bottom of the story, the reporter referenced Dr. Hampton, the oncologist at Baptist Medical Center. I went to the hospital, where I approached him in the hallway. "Tell me about the hospice," I said.

He gave me some contacts for the administration, but he also provided me with the name of a businessman from Dallas who was opening another hospice in the community with his wife, a licensed practical nurse.

Carol and Rocky Reece were coming to town with another woman who would run the hospice during the startup. We went to dinner at a Chinese restaurant and discovered, to our mutual delight, that we had the same vision and goals. In other words, we clicked. They provided lessons in the hospice business that were just what I needed. Then, in 1991, they sent me to Georgetown University to a national conference on hospice. I soaked it all up like a thirsty sponge.

It was at that first hospice that I learned the value of morphine and the correct way to use opiates for managing pain. It was pivotal learning that is sadly still absent in medical education today and has been missing long before the opioid crisis became big news.

My commitment to hospice involved a meeting every week or two with an interdisciplinary team (IDT), which included social workers, nurses, chaplains, and volunteers—basically anyone involved directly in hospice patient care. My only issue with seeing patients was my time. I usually saw them after hours or on weekends, but for the most part, the nurses communicated with the team about their care and needs. When I started, I had to make personal visits every sixty days for the patients' recertification in order to attest that their clinical course was essentially on a decline and their prognosis was six months or less if they progressed as medical science predicted based on their diagnosis and associated diseases. Patients were required to be certified upon admission, then recertified after ninety days, and then every sixty days indefinitely, providing they declined clinically.

I reviewed patients' histories, examined them, and talked to them (my favorite part), usually at length. I also talked to the families and almost immediately had to ask difficult questions like, "Why are we doing this? What do you hope to get out of it?"—and quite a few more that let me know the extent of their denial or acceptance in a process referred to as a patient's "goals of care."

Home visits were often beautiful and, occasionally, very hard. Sometimes, I would run into overwhelming denial. I had one particularly memorable case. The patient lived about a mile from our place in a huge house off Route 66 next to the lake. Karen and I had driven by the house a number of times, admiring the big, white house with pillars at the front, looking like a southern antebellum plantation mansion. Karen and I would often look at each other, saying, "Wouldn't it be cool to live there?"

I walked into that imposing house to see the patient, the man who had designed and built it. The big double doors opened to a dual curved staircase that met at the top balcony, looking down at the marble-tiled foyer. The family led me to the master bedroom, where the patient was half sitting against a stack of pillows, awake and alert. I complimented his house while he told me a good deal of its history. I could have talked with him for hours, but I had a job to do.

The patient had prostate cancer and had just been transported home via air ambulance from the MD Anderson Cancer Center with the message, "There's nothing more we can do." He was receiving a blood transfusion every week—occasionally twice a week, but by the end of the week, the blood was gone. In healthy patients, the blood usually hangs around for four to six weeks. Radiation and chemotherapy had trashed his bone marrow. The family was worn out, completely exhausted. His wife, sons, and daughters-in-law were all present when I visited. The patient no longer had the strength to stand by himself, let alone walk anywhere. I realized quickly that the family was hoping I could talk to him about the futility of the steps he was taking and let him know he had the right to stop treatments that were never going to make a difference.

"But I'd be weaker if I didn't have the blood transfusions," he said.

One of his sons said, "Dad, you can't get out of bed now. How much weaker can you get?"

He nodded. I looked closely at him, seeing the lines of pain in his face. The family, too, was in pain, but they were also determined to do what was right. He and the family willingly and gratefully shared all the information they had, including that he had strong religious beliefs and that he had a "do-not-resuscitate" order.

During that lengthy conversation, he said, "I'm not ready to die yet."

I have three rules, and this experience played a role in their creation.

Everyone dies.

God decides.

See rule number two.

We talked about the multiple issues with blood transfusions, tying that into the do-not-resuscitate order. I let him and the family know the statistics of CPR that are not as available as I believe they should be. The fact is that people who have cardiac arrest outside the hospital only do well if all other systems are healthy and functioning normally, which is often not the case.

However, his strong religious beliefs told him that God had the ability to perform miracles. His son quickly pointed out that God does have that power, but He also has the ability to take away pain and suffering by different means. We briefly discussed his beliefs, imagining that his life as a minister would surely lead to his reward, and he agreed this was probably true.

We also talked about the difficulty of the process and concept of faith. After our discussion that day, he made the decision to accept what we called "comfort care measures only," which meant remaining at home with my personal promise to keep his pain, anxiety, and any discomforts at bay.

One thing I realized in hospice work is that do-not-resuscitate orders can be signed by the patient or the family member with power of attorney (POA), but the form can also be signed by the doctor, stating the diagnosis is not one that leads to survival, thus eliminating any guilt the family might feel about giving up and signing what they might believe is a death warrant. I have developed the habit of reminding nursing staff to inform patients and families of my offer to sign DNR forms, and I've been taken up on the offer many times. Too many doctors don't understand what a great kindness and compassionate service it is. Perhaps they are reluctant, fearing it will lead to legal issues or even their own guilty feelings of giving up.

Too many doctors also don't understand the importance of signing death certificates stating clearly the cause of death along with comorbid conditions. Why? The belief that death is failure has been drilled into them all through medical school. I don't see it that way.

The most important thing about death is the end of pain and suffering. I've looked after so many people. One, who was a hundred and four, told me flat out, "I'm mad at God."

"Why are you mad at God?" I asked.

"Because I don't want to be here. All my friends are gone, and I don't have family that comes to see me."

That's what I call suffering.

Over the years, I collected dozens upon dozens of stories from hospice—stories that have stayed in my heart.

An 89-year-old veteran and grandfather of a well-known college football player was one of my patients. He was a WWII veteran and Native American who had been in and out of the hospital every month for about half a year. Every time he arrived at the hospital, he was given a swallow test, and he passed it every time—until now when, I was called in to see him.

Not passing the test meant he was at risk for aspiration—swallowing food or liquids and aspirating them into his lungs. The hospitalist told him they would "have" to insert a feeding tube. He said, "No, you're not. I don't want a feeding tube."

"Well, sir," the doctor said. "If we don't put that feeding tube in, your risk of aspirating goes up. It can even lead to death."

He said, "I don't care. I do not want a tube or artificial feeding. Leave me alone."

As I see it, there is also a risk even higher with the feeding tube, which statistically increases the risk of aspiration as well.

Every month, when he was discharged, he was taken back to a skilled nursing facility (SNF) under the naive assumption he would get stronger. Why? A month later, he was back. This time, the hospital had asked an intake nurse from hospice to see him and she called me because the hospice administrator had denied his transfer to inpatient hospice. Laura, the intake nurse, said, "Steve, will you come by and see this patient? I think he's really appropriate for the inpatient hospice unit, but the powers that be don't agree."

I referred to this as the "gauntlet of admission"—inpatient beds being reserved for patients rapidly approaching death, sometimes within hours or days. We only had twelve inpatient beds, so we had to follow somewhat rigid standards.

They didn't think he was going to die imminently, but how could they make that assumption without seeing him? Why would they deny his transfer?

I went to the hospital the next day and spent about twenty minutes looking through his chart. He had a "do-not-resuscitate" order and an advance directive saying he did not want a feeding tube. When I talked to his daughter, she said, "It's his decision. I'll stand by him."

I spent almost two hours with him and his daughter, as I did with every patient about to be admitted, talking about what the Hospice House was, what it did, and why we sent people there frequently because their pain was difficult to control and they needed comfort care measures. He listened, saying very little.

"Do you have any pain?" I asked.

He crossed his arms and leaned back against the bed. "No."

After our discussion, his daughter and I left the room, and as we started down the hall, I had a thought. He wasn't going to admit to pain in front of his baby girl, even after I'd explained that we could control his symptoms and no procedures were done there, only comfort and what the patient desired.

As we continued to walk, I said to his daughter, "I think I will go back by myself and talk to him after I take care of a bit of paperwork."

She said, "Okay."

"Are you going to be here?"

"Yes. I'll be in the family waiting area."

After taking care of my administrative work, I went back to his room and pulled a chair right up to him—face-to-face. "Sir," I said. "I think what you want and need is what I've got to offer."

I held my finger and thumb up close together. "Can we give you just a little bit of morphine?"

He just looked at me and said, "I want a lot."

"So you're willing to do this?"

"Yup."

"Okay, I'll make the arrangements."

They transferred him that day and he passed comfortably three or four days later, his pride, honor, and dignity intact to the end.

CHAPTER 11

Stories from Hospice

I have so many stories from hospice that I have no hope of remembering them all. Each one is a lesson in caring and empathy that I will always carry close to my heart, each one reminding me that I have been blessed by God.

Wally Brushwood was a guy who would call you a rotten old son-of-a-bitch if he liked you. I first met him in about 1988 when I was trying to figure out exactly what was going on with his wife, Nancy. She was a phenomenal person who had the worst case of rheumatoid arthritis I'd ever seen. She also had bronchiectasis, a kind of chronic bronchitis often associated with rheumatoid arthritis and also often seen in smokers, which she was not. Wally was a heavy smoker, so secondhand smoke likely contributed to Nancy's condition.

I sent her to a chest surgeon in case we needed to take out part of her lung due to severe chronic infection. The opinion came back negative. The surgeon was concerned that removing part of the lung would leave her ability to breathe and oxygenate far too compromised. The lung medical specialist concurred and decided the best option would be aggressive lifelong treatment of the ongoing infection. This meant frequent and creative encounters with Nancy, which in turn meant Wally would be in the driver's seat with her medical care. She lived another forty years. He followed orders very well and really cared about his wife.

One day, Wally showed up at the office and presented me with a rod and reel—as a thank-you, I suppose, because he presented them with the words, "It's the nicest G***D***ed fishing rig they had!" I cherish that gift because I know it came from someone who didn't have a lot to spare. He and Nancy lived in a trailer and for work, Wally could turn his hand to just about anything. He was a "good old boy" who was there when you needed him and could always be counted on to help a neighbor out.

The first time Karen met him, I was having surgery to repair my diaphragm, which had suffered a bit from my esophageal surgery. Any time I was ill for more than a day or two, or when I went in for a surgery, rumors that I was dying would spread like wildfire on a dry prairie. On this occasion, the first after my esophageal surgery and moving to Yukon, Wally came to the house and knocked on the front door. Karen opened it and he introduced himself. Then he paced a bit, kicked at a floorboard or two, cleared his throat a few times, and finally said, "Is Dr. Drabek going to be okay?"

Soon after that, we moved to a new home we'd built on two lots in a new subdivision. Ours was at the back of the neighborhood and the first to be completed. We hadn't bothered developing the back lot. I may have mentioned to Wally at some point that the property was kind of rough. One day, I came home from work to see Wally sitting on his little rototiller/tractor, smoothing out the entire back lot. The tractor looked like it was on its final legs, but it worked.

That was Wally—jumping in and helping where he saw help was needed. And don't even try to repay him! What he did was given freely from his heart and with a sentence that inevitably ended with, "You SOB!"

When he got cancer, he declined rapidly. Just before admitting him into hospice, I called the chaplain at the prison, where his son, Clyde, was incarcerated on a drug charge. I discussed the situation, explained it was terminal, and requested a medical leave to allow Clyde to see his father.

The chaplain's support was critical, especially when he discussed the situation with the Warden. Happily, they gave their approval. I was in the hospital when Clyde walked into his father's room. Wally beamed with joy, and Clyde, all six-foot-four of him, simply crawled into the bed to hold his father close.

Whenever I had a personal patient in hospice, I always told the nurses, "If they're getting anywhere close or are actively dying, let me know."

Wally was staying with his daughter when the nurses told me he was no longer getting out of bed. I went to the house and went straight to his room, where I sat on the edge of the bed. We talked for at least an hour, mostly about life in general and also about that wonderful visit he'd had with his son in the hospital. I wanted to make sure he was comfortable—and he was. It was a good talk, rising to a different level of deep understanding.

Finally, I stood and said, "Wally, I have to go."

He looked at me and said, "Steve—God bless you."

I'll never forget those words. I think it was the only time he didn't call me an old son-of-a-bitch."

He died a couple of days later.

His wife, Nancy's death many years later was an especially hard one. She was deteriorating mentally, and I was just glad I could be there for her and for Clyde, who had been out of prison for a while by then.

People like Wally and Nancy meant a lot to me. They were part of my practice. More than that, they were a piece of me.

Robert was a patient in his early nineties. I had just come home from the office when one of the hospice intake nurses called, "Steve, we had a call from someone looking for you. Do you remember a patient called Robert?"

"One hundred percent," I said. He'd lost his wife many years earlier, and his son was a vascular surgeon in the Dallas area. Robert had come into the office fairly regularly, never for anything very serious, but he would tell me how he was feeling and how the loss of his wife had left him broken-hearted. He was like an old friend who needed to visit with me to talk about life in general. Retired from a successful career, he often reflected on life and was eager to share his wisdom. We talked about the end of life and advance directives and how he didn't want any aggressive interference when the time came.

His daughter had found me because Robert had told her about me and our talks. When I called her back, she said, "My dad wants you to take care of him. Is that acceptable?"

"Absolutely."

I discovered that Robert had been in a hospital only a few miles away and had been sent to a skilled nursing facility to get stronger. What an asinine practice! Again! Far too often, patients were sent there with the naive thought they were going to get stronger and have more quality of life even when they were at end-of-life. And so often, all a patient wanted was to go home and die. That's exactly what Robert had told his daughter, and she stood firmly behind his wishes and was willing to care for him at home to the end.

The hospitalist who cared for him had responded to their request with, "You can't go home. We must send you to a skilled nursing facility."

That same afternoon, I visited the facility. I hadn't seen him in three or four years, and he had since lost most of his vision. "Bob," I said. "It's Dr. Drabek. Do you remember me?"

A big smile lit up his face. "I don't want to be here," he said. "My daughter's in town and she's willing to take care of me. I want to go home."

"Then let's get you home," I said.

I contacted the nursing home doctor and we sent him home later that day. I believe he lived another ten or fourteen days. He was able to pass peacefully and rejoin his wife in heaven. His daughter expressed her thanks, and I told her, "The greatest honor for me is when people like Bob seek me out for care on hospice, and I'm willing and able to take care of them."

This is why I tell people I will be involved in hospice until I take my final role as a patient under hospice care unless the concept of "death with dignity" becomes universal throughout the United States, just as it is in other countries.

As a doctor, or even as a human being, I can't make any assumptions about people. I don't know what their goals are unless I ask them. My job is to provide care for people, but only after I understand their needs and desires. I can't know if I only spend ten minutes with them, rushing off to the next patient for another brief impersonal encounter. Contrary to the operating philosophy of our current medical "system," it's not about the money; it's about the patient.

I receive what I personally refer to as the non-financial bonus to providing care: the satisfaction of knowing you are meeting their goals of care and accepting the fact that rule number one applies: everyone is going to die. I hope and pray when I am in that position, someone will listen to me and do the same for me.

Am I unusual in my belief? No. I prefer to be referred to as an anomaly. I also believe I'm not the only one in the medical profession who believes in patient-centered care. However, I also see a lot of lip service given to that concept. It's not about how long you live; it's about your quality of life. Our medical education brainwashes us into thinking that death is the worst thing that could happen. It's not. Skilled nursing facilities used to be a wing of the hospital, but the administrators deemed them cost-ineffective because they left patients without the motivation to improve their own health, vegetating in an expensive profit-generating bed. Now, skilled nursing facilities are wings in nursing homes that prey on people's fear of death. I got a call recently regarding a hospice patient because the facility was concerned about the patient's blood pressure.

Wait! The patient is under hospice care with advanced dementia. What does her blood pressure matter? I asked the nurse, "Is the patient agitated?"

If she's agitated, of course, her blood pressure will be high—and it's not hypertension. It's agitation and could well be what we refer to as terminal agitation, which occurs when a patient is unable to understand or realize what is going on inside themselves, constantly in a state of agitation, and not responding to family or their surroundings. Once they are given appropriate medications by a hospice nurse or an understanding family member, and the agitation calms down, they will pass peacefully. I also make sure all parties involved with this process understand that there will always be a final dose of medication for the patient's comfort. That will be followed by death. It may take minutes or hours, but the medication does not cause death.

Rule number 2: God decides when death occurs. Rule number 3: see Rule number 2.

We have an unreasonable and unreasoned fear of death. Doctors create panic. If you don't give the patient something or do something, they will die! A doctor is rarely present when a patient passes. The one exception I have seen was in the television western "Gunsmoke" when ole Doc was almost always present; he provided to the end, even if just being present.

Rule number one. Followed by rule number two. Then, rule number 3: see rule number 2.

During the COVID pandemic, a brilliant doctor and director of an Emergency Room in New York City took her own life because she couldn't prevent deaths from COVID-19. She was forty-eight. This tragedy exemplifies a problem with medical education, and this is also why hospice is a team approach. Hospice care is specifically designed with support in mind so that all parties involved in patient care are present and able to offer one another support when they are under emotional stress.

That's why I've become what I named myself—a comfortologist. It's the title I tell my pain management patients because that's what it's about—soothing patients and decreasing their fears and anxieties. This is done by appropriately treating their pain.

In the beginning of my hospice years, I worked with an infectious disease specialist who had great compassion for the HIV population and was well-known for her expertise in the field. She once made a comment at a medical committee meeting that she would like to see a support function for physicians when her patients were dying too often, as hers were due to HIV. This was long before our current medications were developed, leading to successful survival in the HIV population. She was told by other physicians to stop getting so close to her patients. She dropped the idea. When I saw her years later, I asked how she was doing. "I'm doing great," she said. "My patients are no longer dying like they were in the past."

Bruce, one of my pain management patients, was a licensed practical nurse (LPN) who initially came to me for pain management. Shortly after his first visit, he was admitted to the hospital, where he was diagnosed with a hugely enlarged prostate. He was not a candidate for surgery. His PSA was over six hundred. Normal is four or less.

He had worked in a nursing home and had a good handle on how the system worked. A friend from Texas visited—his only visitor because he had no family. None. Bruce's friend called me a couple of times and one time, he said, "I want to take him back to Texas. I'm really the only family he has."

I told him what he needed to do. "Get a power of attorney."

"I already did that."

"Good. Then they're going to want to do all kinds of things to Bruce, which Bruce has already told me he doesn't want under any circumstances. You just need to make sure he's comfortable. Find a hospice and keep him at home. You can make him comfortable there, and hospice will help you with that, providing the medications and care for him in the home."

A month or so later, the nurses at the office told me Bruce's friend had called. I called back. "I just wanted to call and let you know that Bruce passed away."

"How did that go?"

"You know what? It went exactly as you said it would—and I am so thankful that you told me everything that was going to happen so I could keep him at home and not cause him more pain and suffering."

Conversations like that always bring tears to my eyes. Bruce was not a particularly charming individual. He was a down-to-earth guy, but everybody deserves respect and dignity, and the dignity comes from doing what they want. For many people, that means not living if they don't have quality of life.

Betty, another pain management patient, was in the Family Practice Residency Program. I can say half-jokingly that if you want to be mistreated, be a residency program patient. I was a resident once. It's part of the learning process, after all.

The residents blamed everything that happened to Betty on the pain medications that were perfectly appropriate for her conditions. They would decrease her pain meds regardless of how much pain she was feeling, if her blood pressure was a bit low, or if she complained about being tired or fatigued.

"Well, that's due to the pain meds."

No. That's her heart failing. Also her immobility leads to fatigue along with pain.

At an office visit one day, I got a bit more of her history, asking questions most medical people never seem to take an interest in. I discovered that she was walking on the streets of Oklahoma City one day when she noticed a Ryder rental truck parked next to the Alfred P. Murrah Federal Building minutes before it blew up. She also saw Timothy McVeigh walking down the street. I continued to probe. She served as a witness in McVeigh's trial, attending every day of his trial in Denver, Colorado. I'm not sure if she attended his execution, but I believe so. That experience was part of her medical history, and we owed her the respect of not tapering her pain meds and blaming them for her health issues.

I wanted her in hospice, but no one in the residency program would even talk to me about coordinating her care. Instead, they kept insisting she was not terminal despite multiple organ diseases and progressive failure. They were only causing her more pain and suffering by prolonging her disease processes, one of which was PTSD. But we owed her a lot for her commitment to justice. She was instrumental in the prosecution's case, yet no one ever mentioned that history to me or documented it in her extensive health record. She deserved the dignity of recognition and management of the pain, whether it was physical, which was quite significant, but also if it was mental suffering, and I suspected that to be absolutely true. I know this from my own experiences of JFK assassination theories, constantly reminding me of my mother's unfortunate death in 1963, just prior to the assassination and days before my mother's birthday.

Another hospice patient was ninety-eight years young. I met him when he married the patient I'd been seeing for twenty years; she was in her late 80's. His issue was rectal bleeding, so I sent him to a gastroenterologist, an English chap, Dr. Paul Maton, who I greatly admired and we had a great relationship. Surprisingly, he refused to do a colonoscopy because he felt the patient was too old.

I called Dr. Maton when my patient gave me the news. "Paul," I said. "This guy's not ninety-eight years old; he's ninety-eight years young! He still works in his garden and has exercised every day since retiring from the military.

"Well then, Steve, you're right," Paul said. "Maybe we should do a colonoscopy."

"Well, yeah!"

He did and found colorectal cancer in the lower part of the colon. They operated with laparoscopic removal of the colon and minimally invasive surgery. The following morning, the patient went home.

Sadly, he was diagnosed with pancreatic cancer six months later and passed rather quickly after that. But still, we bought him six months, and at least four of those were quality.

Doing the right thing for each patient isn't that hard. You just have to think outside the box, and that's what modern medicine can't seem to do very easily. I believe my varied experiences over my lifetime blessed me with many boxes to work out of while also providing the income to get where I ended up in medicine.

Another ninety-two-year-old patient was bleeding in his colon, so he was admitted by the hospitalist. I consulted with him in the hospital after they did surgery. He was not nearly as young as my other older patient. He had an advance directive and had no desire to have surgery even though the hospital was pushing him in that direction, saying he would die without it. His daughters reluctantly agreed to the surgery but were adamant that they did not want him dependent on a ventilator afterward. The operation went okay, but they couldn't take him off the ventilator because his lungs weren't functioning perfectly.

I was called in to see him for a palliative medicine consultation. His daughters were standing by his bed, demanding that the ventilator be taken away while I was outside at the nurses' station, reading his chart. I went into the room, consulted with them, and we were able to take him off the ventilator. His daughters wanted his comfort above all else, so we transferred him to the hospice inpatient unit for comfort only. He remained stable all that day but started bleeding again late that night. The hospice nurse called me the next morning, telling me he had died that night. She said, "This was the worst bleed-out I've ever seen or cared for."

If he had been in the ICU in the hospital, they would likely have performed another surgery. What we did was the right thing based on the patient's wishes, as well as those of his daughters standing firm to support their father's wishes.

However, the nurse practitioner who had called and requested me to see the patient in the hospital pissed off the hospitalist and the pulmonary doctor managing the ventilator. They became even more furious when we sent him to The Hospice House. They reported the nurse practitioner (but not me) to the hospital ethics committee. I didn't know any of this until a month later because the nurse practitioner was told not to talk to anyone about the case.

When I discovered what had happened, I learned that she did not get into trouble for what she had done, but she did not know what had happened to the patient after the transfer to hospice. When I realized I was part of the events but not the process involving the ethics committee, I printed out the discharge summary that I dictated on the transfer and handed it to her one day to relieve her feelings of guilt.

None of these events would have happened if everyone involved had simply followed the patient's requests despite their personal disagreements, outlined in his advance directive and his DNR, and supported by his family.

CHAPTER 12

My Chronic Pain

On a Monday night In late February 1996, I noticed I was having melanotic, or black, stools, indicating the presence of blood. I went home from the office and personally tested my stool. It was positive for blood.

I called my physician, Dr. Don Murray, right away. "Go to the hospital immediately," he said and admitted me that night. By the time I arrived at the hospital, my blood count had dropped moderately. He called the nursing staff in to do a colonoscopy and, if needed, an upper endoscopy. After seeing the results of the blood tests, he ordered them to take me down to the endoscopy lab immediately. The nurses wheeled me downstairs, and as we entered the endoscopy suite, I spotted the bathroom. "I need to go," I said to the nurses.

"Okay," one of them said. "Let me get you a urinal."

"Oh no," I said. "I just need to pee."

Reluctantly, she let me get off the gurney and go into the bathroom. I emptied my bladder and, seconds later, collapsed on the floor. My blood count had gone that low. I woke up to the normally calm and always formal and professional Dr. Murray yelling at me, "Steve, don't you ever do that again!"

He first looked into my stomach with the endoscope and, seeing no sign of bleeding, did what I referred to as the "spin around" for the other end, the colonoscopy. He saw a lot of darkened blood in the colon but no source he could readily identify. Because of my rare and unusual surgical history and probably some good old-fashioned gut feelings, he was convinced the blood was emanating from the upper GI tract, so on Tuesday morning, he did another endoscopy—still no source of blood.

I was getting bored in the hospital, so when Dr. Murray did his rounds Tuesday night, I said, "Hey, Don, how about I go home? I can rest better in my own bed." I will always remember his fatherly response, one that I heard more frequently than I should admit.

"We'll talk about it in the morning."

At about 10.30 p.m. that Tuesday night, I started feeling off—almost like a wave of my dumping syndrome was washing over me. I wondered if that was what was going on. The nurse came in and checked my blood sugar, took my blood pressure, and talked to Dr. Murray.

Everything seemed fine.

On Wednesday morning, my brother, who was an accountant at the hospital, came by to check on me. "How're you doing?"

"I just don't feel right," I told him. Then I went into the bathroom and passed a toilet full of bright red blood. And what should I have done? Leave it. And what did I do? I flushed it.

Fortunately, because of the large drop in my blood count, Dr. Murray had no difficulty believing me. What I didn't know was that my blood count had just about bottomed out.

The nurses wheeled me back to the endoscopy suite early that Wednesday morning. But again, Dr. Murray found nothing. Next, he ordered a tagged red blood cell study where they drew blood, labeled it with a radioactive isotope, and gave it back to me. Then, they used a radioisotope camera to better localize where the leak was occurring in my bizarre GI tract. "Now, Steve," Dr. Murray said. "You're going to the ICU and you're not going to get out of bed."

The nurse that day was given strict orders for ICU Room 901, bed number three and she held the line, no matter how much I ribbed her, even calling her nurse Ratchet, but always with a smile on my face.

A number of my fellow physicians visited me that day, each concerned and fearful of what could happen.

I even had a visit from Stanley Hupfeld, the CEO, after someone mentioned to him I had "taken a turn" that morning. Oddly enough, I was probably the only one who had no fears—not until it was all done and I began looking back. I had complete confidence in Don Murray. He had a reputation for being the doctor's doctor and still does to this day.

Late that afternoon, Dr. Murray gave me the tagged red cell study results. "It looks like the blood is coming from the upper GI tract." It was probably coming from the stomach, which had been customized and lay in the back of my chest area behind my heart, not easily reached surgically. But we didn't see a definite bleeding source. Don Murray frowned at me and said, "We are going to look one more time. If we don't find anything, you may wake up in surgery."

"Don," I said. "I don't want to wake up in surgery."

"You know what I mean."

Then he said, "We will use a pediatric colonoscope, which is longer since it is normally used for a child's colon. Because it's longer, we can go farther down beyond the stomach into the small intestine looking for the source of bleeding."

"Well, Don," I said. "That's really kind of a shitty thing to do."

He rolled his eyes, not even cracking a smile, while his nurse, Nancy, snickered while rolling the endoscope equipment into my ICU room for the procedure to begin.

When Dr. Murray inquired who to use for any surgical issue that might arise, I named my general surgery friend, Dr. Robert Cooke, who also said, "We really do not want to operate on things like this. We hope it can be dealt with endoscopically."

Dr. Murray went all the way down as far as he could with the pediatric colonoscope, finding nothing. He then backed out very slowly, looking at every millimeter along the way. Finally, he noticed a tiny red dot. When he touched it with the end of the scope, it started pumping blood vigorously. He cauterized it within an inch of its life. I still have the picture he gave me of blood pumping out of the anomaly called an artery of Dieulafoy, named after the French doctor who originally described it as a rarely found anomaly. I came to know this on a personal basis. The medical condition is characterized by a large tortuous artery, usually in the stomach wall, that erodes and bleeds. I later added to the definition of this uncommon vessel as the one that only bleeds when not being observed.

Early the next morning, I was still in ICU but somewhat stable when Dr. Murray came behind my privacy curtain with his always present nurse, Nancy, waiting outside with endoscopy equipment at the ready, probably thinking she was being sneaky. "Steve," he said. "I think I cauterized it well, but..."

"Don," I interrupted. "You can look again. I don't have any problem with that. Don't even question it. Just do it." I'd had upper endoscopy work done so many times I'd stopped keeping score. He looked and cauterized the cauterized portion from the day prior just to be sure.

That day, February 29, 1996, I received ten units of blood because my hemoglobin had dropped down to three when the normal was fifteen. That cauterized dot was the beginning of my chronic pain due to so much blood loss. When I started walking, which was pretty much right away, my legs began hurting with a deep, constant ache. "Oh, it's just your bone marrow kicking into high gear to replace the blood you lost," was the general consensus, including that of Dr. Geister, my hematologist. It sounded perfectly rational and all indications were that it would be short-lived and resolve itself as soon as the anemia was corrected.

But the pain never went away, although it did wax and wane. Twenty years later, I was again blessed with the ability to donate another body part. This time, I developed osteomyelitis in the tip of the last bone of my third toe on my right foot. The MRI of the foot clearly showed infection in the distal bone of the right middle toe, less than a centimeter long. They amputated that, but the MRI showed significant small vessel disease throughout the foot and lower extremity.

The orthopedic surgeon explained it was probably a result of the blood I had lost twenty years earlier. When your blood count drops that low, it is shunted to the central vital organs, thus avoiding major organ damage, and the microscopic vessels surrounding the nerves in the lower extremities are shut down, usually for a short time, but mine must have gone haywire longer. And that finally explained what was the most likely cause of my chronic leg pain that nobody seemed to care about since no abnormality was visible. I was thrilled to prove I was not crazy after all. That marked another turning point in my medical career, as I became increasingly interested in the issue of irreversible chronic pain syndromes.

The pain I started feeling after nearly bleeding out that day in February 1996 was nerve pain, and I've reluctantly had to take pain medication ever since. There is no question that medicine saved my life by stopping the blood loss, but it also gave me something that impacted the rest of my life. It gave me many firsthand lessons, showing me that quality of life is more important than quantity. Now, in 2025, I look back and realize that the events I survived through experience were actually blessings that had a firm hand in shaping my professional career. I had found my passion. But the "Big Guy" was not finished with me yet.

In 1990, I learned the art of managing chronic pain, chiefly through the hospice nurses educating me around the clock dosing about the use of morphine and other medications proven throughout history. Medical education had only driven home the issue of drug abuse and misuse, but now I also needed pain control and management. Before that, I had done what I'd been taught in medical school, where we learned about pain from surgical interns: demerol PRN (as required), and may add phenergan to enhance pain relieving effect and duration. And eventually, all pain goes away—true for some surgical pain, but chronic pain does not leave and it can be invisible as well.

I had days and nights when constant pain drove me bonkers. Looking back, I can see that I was disruptive, not to my patients or partners, but definitely to the hospital administrators. We have to understand how dramatically chronic pain can affect a person's life—and the lives of those around them.

It was another personal lesson, which at times left me wondering, "Who is the guy we call God and what the heck is going on?" I look back at the person I was at that time in my life and really don't like who I was or the person that the pain turned me into. However, I never once misused my medication, searching instead through the medical literature for that magic procedure or the answer to why I had pain. It didn't seem fair. But, there is not a magic procedure for many chronic pain issues.

But I remember looking after a family where the mother had a cyst on her spinal canal, and her two sons had chronic pain, one who'd had polio as a child, similar to my granny, and the other with a neurological condition called Brown-Séquard syndrome from a gunshot accident, leaving one side of his body with no sensory perception. The husband, who I did not take care of, had had a heart transplant. Was that fair?

In 2019, a man named Rodney Krueger came to see me and insisted on telling me many hellacious tales about all the things that had been attempted and failed and injections that were not helpful in stopping his pain. I finally had to say, "Rodney, stop. I don't do injections. I use medications. I hear you. I believe you. Let's treat your pain."

He put his head down and wept. Chronic pain stories are everywhere. You'll find them coming from the mouths of drug addicts and mostly from ordinary people. And I tell those patients, "We manage pain; we don't eliminate it." Rodney and I still stay in touch because he continues to have difficulty finding a physician who will continue medications at the dose we found helpful to him. That dose allowed him to construct a small home for himself because his pain was under control. That's no longer happening because they reduced his meds by about seventy-five percent, which led to other bizarre occurrences, probably due to the pain and lack of control. He has also been told many lies about his pain and is undergoing procedures to look for something to fix while not treating his pain, in my opinion.

If you go to a doctor with pain, and he says to you, "Here's what we'll do..." patients seem to assume that whatever the person is proposing will take the pain away. I have always made it clear, "We're not going to take it away. If we're lucky, we're going to make it tolerable." At times, I just tell them to look up the word chronic in good 'ol Webster, and they'll find it says constant, habitual, or continuing a long time or recurring frequently. I also began asking them if anyone could do a better job than God has done. The answer is always no. Medicine or surgery does not fix the problem. Sometimes, they can repair it, but it is not like the original equipment.

Every human being deserves to be treated with care, respect, and dignity. They also deserve to be heard and listened to, which begins with believing them, at least to a point.

One problem is giving patients too low a dose of pain medication on the assumption it will help. Indeed, it might, but the only way to judge the pain relief is through communication. We tend to base our judgments on our education or, in my case, experience with having pain, so again, I am an anomaly. When patients ask for more medication for pain reduction, they appear to be begging or demanding. The medical providers are educated to believe and accuse chronic pain patients that they are addicted, thus creating a judgmental approach of accusations and mistrust.

If they really are addicted, then by definition, their life revolves around the drug, but more importantly, the social structure of their life is destroyed. They lose their job, their marriage, and their family, putting everything else aside to get more drugs. Dependence does occur when people take medication appropriately, and if it's taken away abruptly, they develop abstinence syndrome, better known as withdrawal. This is not addiction. If their pain syndrome can be relieved without medication, people would prefer the alternative and not take medication every day forward, and this includes me.

Recreational drug use is a different animal, and that is where tolerance develops. We see it played out in Hollywood with addicted movie stars and other people in the public eye. But miseducation is a huge problem, and everyone seems to be an expert. Doctors today think that patients taking pain meds daily, even when taking them correctly, will become addicted. Recreational drug use is a crisis in the U.S., but chronic intractable pain is an even larger issue, and in the name of the opioid crisis, it remains largely unaddressed.

Chronic pain has nothing to do with the opioid crisis, but that's difficult to understand unless you have pain that does not go away. If you have chronic pain, the everyday events we take for granted are impacted and become difficult. Chronic pain requires the use of medication around the clock consistently, as opposed to PRN or as-needed dosing. Electronic medical records always put prescriptions for pain in that format—take as needed for pain. It's true that your emotions, lack of sleep, and stress have an effect on pain, whether it is acute or chronic, but there is nothing fun about pain medications in the chronic pain population. We just want relief in the form of regular dosing (around the clock) to keep it at bay. I use the example of the tortoise and the hare—that damn turtle wins every time.

I always tell my chronic pain patients that we all have good and bad days for a variety of reasons, but if you suffer from chronic pain, the fluctuations are more frequent, and dramatic ups and downs occur. We must find ways to cope with pain even when controlled with medications; it is vital. Exercise through a daily walking routine, within each individual's limitations, is critical but can be difficult to initiate. Bottom line: we all have good days and bad days, but staying consistent with medications, activities, and life in general is the key to surviving a life with chronic pain.

The first step to treating any disease is to take a history and do a physical exam. A person with chronic pain has historically had trauma, whether surgical, medical, or emotional. The medical world wants to target emotion as a reversible cause. "Get over it" is heard frequently, but calling them an addict just adds more to their trauma because we are not listening or we are reading between the lines. I sometimes struggle with people needing to get over it, especially when they rate their pain as a 12/10 with a smile on their face. Being consistent and patient with these patients is essential.

I sometimes want to use a line from *Dragnet,* a 1960s TV show where Sergeant Friday would say, "Just the facts, ma'am." But the most important thing is spending face to face time with patients—and time is our leading problem. Doctors rush to see more patients in less time to generate more financial reimbursement. The point is you can bill based on time spent and the complexity of the problems, but hardly anybody wants to deal with complex, difficult problems. And that doesn't serve the patient.

CHAPTER 13

I'm Done

In 2013, I began a consultation service at Baptist Hospital as the Medical Director for Palliative Care Services, in addition to handling daily care for inpatient hospice at the Integris Hospice House. In February 2014, I started working full-time at my absolute dream job: inpatient palliative care at Integris Baptist Medical Center and daily care for patients at the Integris Hospice House. It was what I had always wanted to do in medicine, and I loved it.

The time I spent in that role was full of stories, most of them positive and heartfelt. One of them was a defining moment in palliative care and emotional pain, leading me to a perfect end-of-life experience.

Bill (not his real name) was an eighty-five-year-old patient admitted to the advanced cardiology service, better known as the heart transplant service. He was clearly near the end of his life, but still, the doctors were charged with doing everything they could to prolong it with all the advanced procedures in their playbook. With each option they presented to him, he said, "I don't want any of that."

Dr. Carrie Eshelbrenner, one of the cardiologists, recognized his condition and wishes and helped him sign his do-not-resuscitate order—and that was both unusual and admirable because cardiac doctors are not prone to admitting "defeat." She called me in for a palliative consultation, and I went by to see him on a Wednesday. One of the things he told me repeatedly was, "I'm done." He was absolutely clear about that extremely important message.

The policy in the cardiac department was to evaluate each patient who qualified for an artificial pump called a left ventricular assist device (LVAD) until they could have a heart transplant if they met the criteria for one. If they didn't qualify for a transplant, they would become a destination patient, which meant leaving the pump in and continuing to follow up with them until they died. Many patients in Destination Programs have extended lives for months or even years with many programs around the nation. These programs are approved by Medicare and CMS, and it is remarkable what they accomplish every day. In the meantime, they did everything possible to keep the patient alive in the high-risk environment of an artificial heart pump in the body.

Bill didn't want any of that. He continued to say, "I'm done." All LVAD patients were prone to many complications, which could frequently impact their quality of life. For some, the procedure went well. I had a chronic pain patient whose husband had an LVAD and I would never have known if he hadn't told me. I felt a bit embarrassed because he accompanied his wife to every visit, disguising the bulky battery so well that I never noticed. When he finally told me, we laughed about his skills at going incognito.

It appeared that Bill's goal was to die in the hospital. His family had started to gather around, and one of his sons told me why his father had ended up there. The story went like this:

Bill was best friends with his next-door neighbor who he'd been having dinner with every week for forty years. The neighbor had become ill and gone into a nursing home. For months, Bill visited with him every day. The neighbor had no family, and when he died, he made Bill the executor of his estate, leaving everything to him.

The story provided me with valuable information. Was Bill done with life because his friend was gone?

I entered Bill's room, prepared to give him my usual one or two-hour consultation time. During the course of our conversation, I told him that his son had filled me in on the story of his friendship with his neighbor. Bill shook his head. "I'm going to tell you the real story," he said. "It was forty years ago. My wife and I had just bought a new car."

That's curious, I thought. I wonder where this is going.

"We were both as happy as could be," Bill continued. "We were excited. We picked up the new car and went home and talked briefly and said, 'Let's go somewhere!'"

His wife got behind the wheel and drove through Oklahoma City and then onto Interstate 40, heading east to Shawnee, about forty-five miles distant. In Shawnee, they parked and walked around a bit, enjoying the town before driving back. They were on the interstate heading home when she turned to him with a big smile.

Bill paused. "I can still see that smile today."

"I'll bet you would like to drive, wouldn't you," his wife said.

Bill recalled that they both laughed, and he said, "Sure, if you want, I can drive."

She pulled over to the side of the highway, still chuckling. He got out of the passenger side door and walked around toward the back of the car. She opened her door, got out, and...

Wham!

A car hit and killed her.

I could see the anguish on his face as he told the story—still—after forty years, the pain was as raw as if it had happened yesterday.

When he left the scene that day, he went home as a single dad to three kids. He'd lost the love of his life. He couldn't burden his children with his grief, so he turned to his neighbor, who became his sounding board and friend. Over the years, his dependence on his neighbor grew. He was the person Bill could share his thoughts and feelings with, knowing he would be heard and understood. Losing him may well have echoed the pain of losing his wife forty years earlier. I fully understood what he meant when he said, "I'm done."

But I told Bill, "If the heart transplant cardiologist is unable to do the procedures and evaluation for their advances in cardiac medicine, and they accept your 'I'm done,' then we will not be able to sit idle in the hospital because their services are so specialized. We need an alternate plan. Hospitals are for actions, and I understand you're done."

I explained how the inpatient Hospice House, off the hospital campus, could fulfill his wishes while maintaining his comfort. I mentioned the other option of home care, but it was less desirable because he was practically bed-bound due to his weak heart pumping at about 5-10 percent of normal.

"So, we must do something," I said. "You're not going to be able to stay in the hospital."

When I went back to see him on Thursday, he held firm that he was not going to have any interventions. "Let's wait one more night," he said.

Clearly, he was hoping and praying that he would die in the hospital. But you don't die easily while you're a patient in the advanced cardiology services ward. Understandably, they saw Bill as taking up a bed from someone who could have benefitted from their unique services.

Before leaving that day, I reminded Bill about the inpatient hospice unit, knowing it could be difficult for patients and families to understand before being admitted. Again, he said, "Just one more night is all I want."

Friday came and we had the discussion again. "You're going to be comfortable there," I said. "What we do is what you want, which is comfort and support. I'll guarantee we'll take good care of you." I went on to say that nobody ever asked to be returned to the hospital.

Again, he said, "I'm done."

Dr. Eshelbrenner joined the discussion at the end, confirming my facts about hospitalization. We agreed that one more night would be all right, and we would move him on Saturday.

That weekend was not my time to be on-call, but I told Bill I would come in for the transition, keeping him from having to tell his story over again to the Hospice House on-call physician.

When I left the floor that Friday, I rode down in the elevator with Dr. Eshelbrenner. She listened to my briefing and said, "Okay, but tomorrow, we have to have a plan."

I looked at her and said, "Don't be surprised if he passes tonight."

Her head went up and she had a look of total surprise staring at me. Was she shocked?

"You know," I said. "He could very easily not survive until tomorrow." I believed his hope and prayer to die before Saturday could well be answered.

But he was still alive and awake when I arrived at the hospital early Saturday morning to make the arrangements. While we waited for Bill's transportation, I went ahead to the Hospice House, where Bill's entire family was already waiting in the family room. I talked with them for two hours, listening to their stories and admiring their staunch support of their father's wishes. They stood behind him completely. Once the transport arrived and the nursing staff got him admitted, I decided it was time to see how he was doing. They had put him in room number nine, which frequently housed my special patients.

I entered his room, took his hand, bent down close to him, and asked, "Bill, are you comfortable? Do you think you'll like it here?"

He just gave me a big smile—and that was all the answer I needed.

Then, squeezing his hand with both of mine, I bent even closer. "I told you so," I said, as we both smiled and understood one another completely.

We laughed. I told him the nurses were there to help him. "If you've got pain, we've got medicine. If you're anxious, we've got medicine."

When I arrived at Hospice House early Monday morning, Bill was not there. He'd passed peacefully and with dignity, comfort, and surrounded by family. He'd got his wish. He was done. I was honored to have shared that experience with him and his family. This was what God had given me the desire and drive to do. Death can and should be a pleasant, rewarding event as a physician depending on events surrounding the death. For patients with loving families who understand and support the reality of the situation as well, celebrating a life well lived.

I am so proud of that story. I cherish the memories of the love and respect his family showed him, and even today, I am still touched by the love surrounding that man.

Bill taught me that when someone says to me, "I'm done," I need to listen and believe them if all the other facts are consistent. Yes, some people will use that expression for the wrong reasons, but it's easy to tell the difference. God was done with Bill, allowing him to rejoin his true love.

There was another lesson in Bill's story. The hospital is not the place to die. They don't want you to die there. Their objective is to return you to health when that is possible. Bill didn't want to be probed, and he didn't want IV fluids or experimental protocols and procedures that would postpone death. He wanted company and he wanted to die with dignity and pride. When a patient is at that point in their life, the families that accept it and embrace it are doing themselves and their loved ones a beautiful service. Bill's family made a difficult job for hospice easy by allowing him to have a "good death." He was comfortable, surrounded by his loved ones.

His family was supportive, and people need to know how important that support is. One of my jobs was to convey that and to let them know how important it is to honor a family member's end-of-life decisions. That is the most loving and compassionate thing they can do for their loved one.

Bill needed a guide for a complicated journey to bring finality with meaning through understanding to the difficult path he followed on this earth. I was lucky enough to be a part of his precious journey at the end, for which he wanted a voice because he knew the direction by heart.

CHAPTER 14

Hospice

I have so many stories like Bill's. I also had patients who were the exact opposite. There were occasions when I was escorted out of the room, but I always told people, "There is no right or wrong way to do this." My decisions were always based on a patient's personal goals of medical care. Family members sometimes did not discuss these goals with their loved ones.

When discussing palliative care, many people would tell me they had no idea they could question the treatment they were receiving or even refuse it. "I didn't know that 'no' was a potential response."

It seemed that doctors in the hospital setting had begun to resist the process of listening to the patients and honoring their wishes. I had a patient with end-stage lung disease under the care of Dr. Bill Cook, one of the best pulmonary doctors I've ever known. One day, I said to him, "Bill, you do too good a job managing these people with end-stage lung disease."

He knew exactly what I meant. One of his patients knew he was dying from advanced lung cancer and wanted to go home. Dr. Cook said, "If we can get your oxygen level up to ninety or higher, you can go home."

But the patient had stage IV lung cancer, and cancer gets the first shot at all the nutrients entering the body, so the tumor grows, which is why cancer makes patients lose weight for reasons not obvious until the cancer is widespread. There was absolutely no way his oxygen level was going to meet Dr. Cook's desired target. Hospital oxygen systems can give ten liters of oxygen, but at home, the portable concentrators max out at five liters. In the Hospice House, we had concentrators, not a central oxygen supply. Dr. Cook, being diligent and tenacious, hated to give an inch, but he agreed that if Hospice House would take him, he'd allow the patient to be transferred there.

We transferred him, but still—he simply wanted to be home with his family and his dogs. The day after transferring him, we sent him home, and he passed a few days later. That was another proud moment for me because we honored the patient's wishes (sorry, Bill).

I remember a federal judge, a man who issued orders and expected them to be followed. He was in the same ICU where I'd been when I'd had my gastrointestinal bleed. He was on BiPap, a non-invasive ventilator treating his respiratory failure, and he was aware of his prognosis. He couldn't eat or drink, and he was raising hell. When I went to see him, he was so angry I could barely get him to talk to me. When I finally settled him down, I said, "I'm here to help you."

"I want to go home," he grumbled.

"Okay, that's what we're going to do."

"They said I can't go home."

"I will go ahead and make arrangements for you to go home with hospice today."

His daughter, who was there from out of town, was completely on board. She knew her father wasn't going to stop raising hell until he got what he wanted (and deserved). I sent him home with hospice, and he died exactly where he wanted to be.

I listened to my patients' wishes every single time. When a patient asked, "What do I have to do to get out of this hospital?" My answer became, "You have to raise hell at the nurses' station."

They almost always raised an eyebrow at me. *Huh?*

"If you're out of bed at the nurses' station and visible, you're more likely to go home. If you lay around in bed, it's not likely to happen."

Basically, I was reworking the old maxim, "The squeaky wheel gets the grease," and I was only half joking. But the people who need to go home and should go home aren't sent home because the doctors feel they are in control.

They're not.

See rule number two.

The hospital administration caught on quickly enough. If they had a patient they wanted to get out of the hospital, they said, "Call Dr. Drabek." The fact is, what I was doing was the right thing to do, based on the patient's and family's wishes.

The problem was there were people who were not strong enough to advocate for themselves, or their families did not agree with their decisions. I remember talking to a patient one day who didn't have much time left when his partner burst into the room, yelling at me, "What the hell are you doing here?"

Then he got his face right into his partner's face. "Do you just want to die? You can't just die! You gotta fight!"

I quietly left.

You can read dozens of obituaries talking about a person's brave battle with whatever disease they had succumbed to per the obituary. Notices like that are the story of a tormented human being based on their battle with a disease or condition.

I prefer stories like that of another patient who wanted to get out of the hospital rather than submit to invasive treatments. His sister told me all he wanted was to get out of the hospital and take his grandchildren fishing one more time. We got him home with hospice and a couple of weeks later, his sister sent me a photo of him with the kids on a fishing pier. I still treasure that image, having facilitated his desire with the help of hospice.

Inpatient hospice was not always as heart-warming. My job was admitting the patients, but one day, the administration did it without notifying me, and transfers should be between physicians as a courtesy. The patient at another hospital had been brutally attacked, either stabbed or shot by his own son. He had chest tubes on both sides, and he was not going to survive the attack despite all the futile procedures he had been put through. The son had not been captured.

I got a call from the nurse at the Hospice House who was taking care of admitting him. She'd been told the whole story by the ambulance crew who had transported him, including that the man's son was still at large. The entire Hospice House staff was understandably frightened, wondering if the son had plans to finish the job. The Hospice House was a locked unit, but we weren't equipped to stop bullets, and we had no on-site security guards, so I went immediately to the unit.

In my estimation, the nurse was legitimately afraid. And strictly from a medical standpoint, there was no reason for him to be in an environment with no trained security guard on site. The transferring hospital had obviously just dumped the patient on us because they didn't want him and probably felt we had security on site. I told the nurse to call the ambulance to transport him back to the discharging hospital.

Maybe that's one of the reasons they terminated my contract. I don't care if that was the justification because I did what I felt was right. My priority that night was the staff at the Hospice House. But I was never told why I was dismissed.

In September 2016, I went to the Dominican Republic on my only vacation in the past three years. A week after I returned, I was called to a meeting at the hospital at 8 a.m. I completed two consultations before arriving at the meeting on time.

"We're changing our strategies," they said. "Your services are no longer needed. You'll be paid through the end of your contract in December. Do not go to your office in the medical office building."

"I can't leave," I said. "My keys and some of my personal belongings are in the office."

"Then you'll need to come back tonight."

"I can't leave," I repeated. "I need my keys to drive!"

I called the doctors I'd been consulting with earlier that morning to tell them why I was leaving and that, unfortunately, I could no longer help them. They'd have to talk to the patients' families themselves.

My next stop was the small complex where I had my office. Every door was closed. I focussed on getting a few of my things, but I was furious and had been from the minute they'd told me I was terminated. My anger built and built. At the very least, I deserved to know why. And now to shun me like this—to have security tell the other staff to keep their doors shut and not interact with me! It was shameful.

I went back that night with instructions to call security when I arrived. But I still had my badge, so I went to the office, got my things, and left. Two days later, I made arrangements to meet the manager at the Hospice House to get my personal belongings, but I was not allowed to go to the Hospice House. Instead, I met her in the parking lot of the Cancer Center a mile away where she brought my books and personal effects. By then, I was also feeling much calmer.

Never once did anyone tell me why. But I believe it was because I interrupted a stream of revenue. One thing I did consistently was remove people from life support, including ventilators, which would result in ending a billing of about $10 thousand a day (at that time). However, I only took people off ventilators when I was asked to by their doctors at the urging of the patients' family members because they knew that all hope for quality of life or survival was gone.

No matter—administrators are bottom-line people. At the time, I was angry, furious, frustrated, hurt, and even resentful. Now, I can see that God had a better plan for me. That also fell under His wicked sense of humor and testing my Faith, I suppose.

Twenty minutes after I was dismissed, Karen called me. The father and son who had built our house lived down the street. The father, Bob Russell, was ninety-six and on hospice services. Karen had been sitting with them that morning and had to leave, so I drove straight to their home. In the interim, he passed. Arriving at their home, I called the hospice nurse to report the death. "We've been told not to interact with you at all," she said.

"Look," I said. "This is my personal patient and my friend, and there is no way in hell I'm leaving. If I'm here, that's not your fault."

As far as the hospital administration was concerned, Bob was their patient—not mine. I didn't care about corporate America at that point. Bob and his son, Richard, were close friends and Bob had been a patient under my care for twenty years. When he stopped driving, Bob would occasionally deliver tomatoes to us on his riding mower. What a sight! Bob was a medic in

WWII and went ashore at Normandy, went through 5 major battles, and survived. Bob Russell had lived a full, satisfying life. He had dignity until the end, so being there for the family was an honor. Again, God Wink.

God got me out of that job to be there for Bob and Richard. He also directed me to my next mission, doing chronic pain management and outpatient palliative care.

I started interviewing for jobs right away, going to work for Deaconess Hospital in May 2017 in primary care. I also began outpatient pain management in that practice since the need was and still is quite significant. In the summer of 2018, Integris, my old employer, bought Deaconess Hospital and its outpatient practices. I was given enough of a heads-up to leave in time, starting a new job at St. Anthony's Hospital doing outpatient care.

Integris clearly held a grudge. Understandable, I suppose. I was no shy retiring violet. I was outspoken when I saw the needs of the community. I was probably at my most vocal when I suffered from chronic pain and no one acknowledged it. I was such a nuisance being so vocal that I had been forced to attend a drug rehab facility in Atlanta to prove I was not impaired. And that got me angrier than all the firings in the world ever could. But looking back, even that had an upside because I saw a side of chronic pain I did not want to be a part of—not as a prescriber and not as a person with chronic pain. The danger lies in the risk of addiction through drug abuse. But I proved easily that was not the case for me, nor would it be. There is a blessing in everything if we will only look for it. I returned from that educational experience with more interest in helping the chronic pain population with appropriate pain management and the correct use of medications.

At Deaconess, I quickly became aware there was a great need for palliative care in medicine, both in hospital as well as outpatient care. They knew it, too, but wouldn't admit it. So I did both primary and palliative care there while also building up quite a chronic pain practice because I was willing and able to do pain management, with the realization that chronic pain management is Palliative Medicine, an incurable condition requiring organized, methodical support for the cause of their pain and living with their pain. A year-and-a-half later, when I moved over to St. Anthony's, many of my patients followed me, and I continued caring for them based on their needs, not on the hospital's drive for income, which appears to be directing medicine more and more.

It was during that time that I came up with the "F" word—the most important concept in life begins with

"F." To answer the raised eyebrows aimed at me by anyone who heard me use the expression, I explained, "That F word is Faith."

While working with St. Anthony's, I met some of the most delightful people suffering from chronic pain. Hearing them and documenting their history, it became obvious to me that they deserved and needed somebody to listen to them and treat their pain with appropriate and adequate medications. Along with medication, they also needed respect and education, for which I shared my own personal experiences. They were grateful for that care, along with my jokes much of the time. They needed very specific education on how to manage the various conditions from which they suffered. I often stated that we manage pain; we do not eliminate it. I also added encouragement, telling them frequently that walking daily would improve their pain and overall health.

I started at St. Anthony's on September 11, 2018. Less than two months later, on November 1, the new Centers for Disease Control (CDC) guidelines for prescribing opioids came into effect. Essentially, it meant that doctors who didn't understand pain meds—and that was most of them—were afraid they would go to prison for prescribing any pain medications. And so, I became overwhelmed with pain referrals, some inappropriate and some completely ridiculous. But the vast majority were delightful people.

The patients understood my pain management scale, although most didn't like it. I used the Indiana Pain Scale, tweaking it slightly with terms like nine out of ten is similar to being eaten by a grizzly bear. Ten is unconscious. With the pain scale, I aimed to eliminate the emotional aspects of pain. I also explained the impossibility of eliminating the emotional aspects. I knew that because I had been living with chronic pain every day for the last twenty-seven years.

The hospital clinics seemed to dump many people on my practice, including the patients of interventional pain doctors who refused to prescribe pain medications in the name of CDC guidelines. Most of the referrals were good people, some even wonderful. I learned quickly to sort the good ones from those seeking drugs. I also gleaned a good deal of information through studying their medical records using the powerful electronic record called EPIC. And they truly were EPIC records, although many physicians did not use them well because they didn't add complete historical data; as they say, the devil is in the detail.

About eighteen months into my stay at St. Anthony's, I stopped doing primary care because doctors continued to refer pain patients to me, some who didn't have true chronic pain—they were simply complicated, and the complications needed a thorough primary care doctor. Also, if patients had pain, but their pain was simple and straightforward, I would see them only for their pain but not for their primary care needs. I was becoming overwhelmed.

By 2019, I made it clear that I was busy with chronic pain.

God also gave me a big wink named Hannah Goodspeed, APRN. She had just completed her Advanced Practice Registered Nurse designation (APRN) and was looking for a job. It turned out to be a perfect fit for an old guy in an office pretty much on his own.

Hannah was a natural who made my job easier. She understood the issues, and her empathy for the patients proved to be outstanding. She caught on to the art of pain management easily and quickly and even showed this old dog some new tricks. We quickly got into a new groove and spent a good deal of time practicing and truly enjoying medicine, especially chronic pain management.

Then, March 2020 arrived, and with it, a little virus called COVID-19, technically SARS-CoV-2.

Covid and Sepsis

COVID completely rocked everyone's world. The offices for medical care became abandoned and health care seemed to disappear. We transitioned into a virtual world, and many physicians' offices became ghost-like while patients felt abandoned.

However, the reality of the management of chronic pain was unique and not understood by the medical community. If these patients were abandoned and stopped taking pain medications, they would suffer withdrawal, technically known as abstinence syndrome. The average physician didn't understand that simple concept, and it was a completely unacceptable option. This may be a factor during that time when overdoses increased by about 25% during the pandemic. People possibly refused their medications and turned to wherever they could find relief, and as I always told patients, "Do not get anything from a guy named Guido on a street corner if you do not know what it is."

We turned to the telephone, talking to patients, keeping up with their medications, and refilling their prescriptions. Hannah was a natural for virtual visits, and I was able to meet my patients' clinical needs with a simple telephone call with all their history in the record and digital submission of scheduled medications was mandatory. Most patients weren't happy about navigating the video calls that were taking over the practice of medicine, but we kept it up until the pandemic began to ease and a COVID-19 vaccine emerged in December 2020.

Because I'd had Chronic Lymphocytic Leukemia since 2008, I was at much higher risk with my compromised immune system, so masking up was essential, along with social distancing. And then the battleground for COVID-19 became the hospital, a brutal situation for the doctors and nurses. Perhaps God got me out of my previous dream job for a reason. His knowledge and wicked sense of humor always shine through (wink wink).

Those were crazy times. Some days, I would see people driving alone in their cars wearing a mask. And one day, a motorcyclist passed me on the highway doing seventy MPH, wearing no helmet but wearing an N-95 mask.

Honestly, the masks seemed a bit much when the facts eventually showed influenza was more deadly than COVID. I focused more on social distancing. The virus was shown to spread through respiratory pathways, but unfortunately, contact paranoia was never formally redacted. Everyone in my office experienced COVID at one time except me. Some of my staff even became quite paranoid. One lost her father to COVID, so it was understandable.

On February 1, 2022, Karen and I had to put down one of our wonderful dogs. Pete was 14, a shepherd-malamute mix weighing in at 120 pounds. He looked like a wolf hybrid but was playful and friendly with everyone. Poor Pete had horrible arthritis and could hardly move. Saying goodbye was heart-wrenching. When I got home from that tearful experience, I developed a fever and tested myself. For the first time in two years, after many negative COVID tests, I tested positive. The experimental drug, Paxlovid, made a difference, but when I ran out of meds, my symptoms returned, though somewhat milder. Over time, I became more fatigued, struggling after the acute disease symptoms faded away. I returned to work after the ten-day mandatory leave from the office and Hannah became even more of a star, allowing me to sign and send prescriptions from home. Starting in 2019, all scheduled medications were mandated to be digitally submitted from my computer to the pharmacy.

And then God stepped in. He must have seen my need for another personal teaching experience and decided I needed to add sepsis to my repertoire. Sepsis is a serious condition in which the body's infection-fighting processes are weakened, causing the organs to work poorly in fighting off infection. Sepsis may progress to septic shock, which is a dramatic drop in blood pressure that can damage the lungs, kidneys, liver, and other organs.

I was home one Saturday morning in March when the disease raised its ugly head. COVID and CLL had weakened my immune system enough that it left room for sepsis to take hold. At the time, I only knew I wasn't feeling well and called Karen, asking her to come home. My neighbors called me at the same time, asking if they could come over for a steroid shot for their fairly severe allergies. I said, of course, they could because my nurse (Karen) was also on her way. I sat waiting for her, feeling worse by the minute. If I tried to stand, the world spun around me. When Karen arrived, she took one look and wrapped my arm in a blood pressure cuff. My reading was 60/40.

"You're going to the ER," she said.

I shook my head. "No, I'll get better." I usually did for the last 40 years, that is.

I didn't win that battle.

She drove me to the emergency room at the local hospital who transferred me to St. Anthony's, where I stayed for five days. Hospitalization in the spring of

2022 was pretty grim, mostly due to COVID-19 and its rules for distancing, no visitors, and no access to the hallways, total isolation. The ER physicians had already done most of the bloodwork, which showed that the sepsis had been caught in the early stages. Initially, they gave me six liters of IV fluids for dehydration and low blood pressure.

I was admitted on a Saturday, and by Wednesday, I was beginning to feel much closer to my usual obnoxious self while hospitalized and asked about going home. I'd been seen by a pulmonary doctor, the hospitalist who admitted me, an infectious disease doctor, a cardiologist, and a hematologist. Of course, the hospitalist believed he was in control, and understandably so. When I'd been in that position, I'd usually send patients home when I thought it was reasonable to trust the patient's understanding of the disease process, but with strict instructions to take it easy. I knew they'd sleep better without interruptions every hour or so. The hospitalist on call that day agreed that I could go home, but I had to have portable oxygen.

I had a long two-week recovery period. In my entire career, I'd only been off one other time for two weeks and that was when my family and I went on an Alaskan cruise. Every other time, even after a major surgery, I'd be back in the office too soon by my own admission. But

I did it for my mental health and for the sake of getting out of the house. I firmly believe that you don't get well by lying around. Your risk of getting blood clots goes up, so I insisted on moving, even if it was just a little bit.

Staying at home was tough on me. Karen was still working, and all I could do was lie back in a recliner. I had a long oxygen hose that allowed me a bit of freedom, so one day, I tried to move some items out of one of the bedrooms because my son, Tyler, and his wife, Jackie, were moving in at the end of the month. Walking from one end of the house to the other exhausted me.

Another day, I decided to walk without oxygen down the fairly long driveway to our mailbox. I didn't get too far before I felt myself going. Luckily, I fell to the left and face-planted on the grass.

During this time, Hannah continued seeing patients at the office. I only had to go online to sign their prescriptions. Then, after two weeks, I was finally able to go back to work half-days, but I was tired all the time. At the end of May 2022, I began thinking about retiring, but my obligations to my patients weighed heavily on me.

At the beginning of June, the administrative friend who had helped me get the position at St. Anthony's came to see me. "Are you going to retire?" she asked. I'd mentioned it to a few patients, and I suppose she must have heard. "If you are going to retire, it's okay."

But my health had improved enough by then that I believed I was going to continue getting stronger. I was still taking Wednesday afternoons out of the office to work at hospice, but I decided to take Fridays off, giving me more days to rest while still signing prescriptions at home.

I continued working, hoping I would get more staff to help ease the load. Unfortunately, the administration thought my practice did not require more than one nurse per provider. Hannah and I actually shared a nurse for a long time. The situation continued to get tougher. I couldn't get a break with staffing, and had to do a lot of the medical assistant's work as well as my own.

By January 2023, I knew I couldn't keep it up. I was losing weight, dropping to 148 pounds from 220. On April 28, 2023, the thirty-five-year anniversary of my surgery at the Mayo Clinic, Karen and I flew to Lake Tahoe for a four-day mini vacation. Within twelve hours, I was in the hospital. When they told me I was experiencing altitude sickness, I didn't believe them. It turned out they were right. Another lesson in objectivity: thank you, God.

Maybe God sent me to Lake Tahoe to experience the wonderful care I received at the hands of the medical staff at their small hospital. They pulled up my electronic medical records, the same ones we used in the major hospitals in Oklahoma City (EPIC), and actually read my chart. I'm convinced the doctor who looked after me studied every word. When he mentioned something from my records, I said, "You read my chart!"

He replied, "Isn't that what we're supposed to do?"

Well, yes, but they didn't do that when I was in St. Anthony's, where they signed me out with a diagnosis of esophagitis, even though I don't have an esophagus.

At the Lake Tahoe Hospital, they put me on oxygen, the usual treatment for altitude issues. We'd arrived on a Friday. On Sunday, I went back to the hotel, and on Monday, we flew home with a portable oxygen concentrator; I was fine as soon as I left the higher elevation.

CHAPTER 16

Retirement

I retired on June 30, 2023. It was hard, but fortunately, some of my strength and endurance had begun to return. My patients gave me many small gifts that meant a lot to me. I couldn't help but think back to a pain management doctor in Arizona who retired in 2017, looking completely done as he walked toward his car in the parking lot for the drive home to his family. And then, he was shot and killed by a patient's spouse because his wife would no longer be treated for pain. I hoped and prayed that was not going to be my story.

Even in 2017, pain management was a crisis. Fortunately, my patients weren't angry. They were upset but seemed to understand. They'd watched me fading away over the past year, losing seventy pounds, most of it muscle mass. I hadn't weighed that since junior high. Many of them would ask about my health issues with genuine concern. I never held back the facts because if you try to hide something, people will either work harder to find out what it is or they'll stop trusting you.

I've stayed in touch with some of my wonderful patients, and I've made attempts to find someone willing to accept them and manage their pain. It isn't easy. I've heard many horror stories of doctors saying they must be tapered off their medications. I've read the CDC guidelines many times, and while they do discuss the possibility of tapering their pain medications, they also specifically state tapering only if appropriate and only if the patient agrees. Nowhere in the guidelines does it say you should treat people like shit.

The CDC website summary states: "This guideline provides recommendations for primary care clinicians who are prescribing opioids for chronic pain outside of active cancer treatment, palliative care, and end-of-life care." As has been stated by the CDC, a recommendation is not a mandate. You simply have to follow the clinical standards by documenting why you did the right thing and being specific with your reasoning. In other words, logical reasoning. By doing this, you're reducing the physician's as well as the patient's risk of adverse outcomes. This means appropriate guidance and counseling for the patient and explaining the risk of opiates if they are used incorrectly.

I've tried talking to the residency program at St. Anthony's, only to learn that they seemed to think all I did was hand out drugs. I sent emails offering my assistance to try to educate the residents and the attending physicians about pain, but those attempts went unanswered. Nobody wanted to talk about pain in any capacity, which made my practice very busy.

I have done many things in my attempts to get help for my patients, including referring them to the home palliative care program when that is appropriate. Usually, the patients were homebound due to illness. I still sign the prescriptions for those with the home palliative care programs with which I am associated. They receive visits from advanced practice nurses under my supervision. The APRNs regularly communicate with me before I sign their prescriptions and send them to the pharmacy. Bottom line: I am committed to doing the right thing for people who truly deserve pain control, as well as being someone who will listen to them.

Medicine has become more and more impersonal, yet it's supposed to be about quality of life and reducing suffering. We cheer for that storyline in the movie *Patch Adams,* where Robin Williams played the famous doctor, but what about real life? I've made house calls my entire career—the perfect way to better understand your patient's situation. How many physicians do that? And is it even the fault of the doctors? In medical training, home visits seem to be reserved for nursing homes.

I recently had eye surgery. Insurance companies have stopped paying if the surgeon operates on both eyes at the same time. They used to pay a thousand dollars for each cataract removal. If they operate on the other eye at the same time, the insurance company has reduced the fee by fifty percent for any additional procedure beyond the primary or first procedure. Previously, if a patient had bilateral inguinal hernias, general surgeons would do both sides on the same day under one anesthetic. When insurance companies started paying only fifty percent for the second operation, doctors began telling people, "We can't do them both on the same day." It's all about reimbursement. However, the most significant risk is anesthesia, which can take a person's life. I know. That's how my mother died. Now, the insurance companies have doubled the risk with two separate anesthetics, not to mention the inconvenience of two separate everythings required for the operation—all in the name of reducing cost!

The hospital administrator's job seems to be doing whatever brings them the most reimbursement. While I understand that, I need to ask, "What about the patient? What's best for them?"

The first time I had a hernia repaired in my diaphragm (I had it twice seven years apart), I asked the surgeon, who was a friend, to also take out my appendix.

The charge for doing that while performing a diaphragmatic hernia operation was a fraction of what it would have been as a stand-alone procedure. At the same time, he also repaired the site where the feeding tube had been placed by Dr. Payne in the event I needed additional nutrition. Thankfully, the feeding tube was never used. It all made economic sense. But if that were a normal practice, it would mean less profit for the hospital as well as the surgeon. Honestly, I don't know if the additional procedures were even billed. However, it was certainly extra work.

Recently, a well-known national insurance company proposed limited anesthesia time for a variety of procedures, but every surgical procedure varies based on many different conditions and potential risk factors. When you have an operation, you do not want someone with a stopwatch standing in the operating room counting down the seconds. I always expected surgeons to work slowly and meticulously, whether I was the patient or the assistant in the operating room. Speed would be fine if every surgery were simple and straightforward. But sometimes, there is the risk of the patient dying because they didn't follow instructions. Maybe they smoked a cigarette while driving to the hospital or ate something beyond the time instructed by the surgeon. They may not have understood that if they ate or drank for the eight hours before surgery, they could vomit and aspirate.

People should be given clear and concise instructions, and that's usually what happens. But too many doctors rely on their assistants to handle that. Some of the doctors and assistants are very good, but others don't understand why they are giving those instructions, or they feel rushed as they do that very important job. When I was recovering from COVID-19, I was on oxygen for more than a year, and they provided me with new tubing every month. So, every month or two, I would get a call from someone at the oxygen supply company asking if I needed more tubing. I didn't change it every thirty days. Instead, I would check it for humidity and moisture. One time, I asked the person who called, "Why do you want the tubing changed every thirty days?"

The person who called could not answer my question. We make assumptions we shouldn't make. Doctors and healthcare workers sometimes assume patients have the same knowledge and education we have. Many don't, but then doctors don't want to be seen as being judgmental.

My experience with the medical community has been that doctors and healthcare personnel, in general, are probably the most judgmental group in our society, especially when it comes to pain medications and chronic pain. They believe these medications lead to addiction and drug abuse, even when taken appropriately. That's what their medical education taught them, and sometimes, they were instructed by people inexperienced with the population suffering from chronic pain. Some patients exhibit only subtle signs of chronic pain, but they do suffer because chronic pain is not often reversible. I reminded my chronic pain patients that nobody can do a better job with the body than God, and still, sometimes, things go awry. Medical education is about average normal physiology, not about those of us who experience anatomical rearrangement or near-death events. I proudly refer to myself as an anomaly of medicine and completely unfixable. But with all the things I have experienced, I see myself as fairly normal physiologically. Anomaly is much better than FUBAR (thoroughly confused, disordered, damaged, or ruined) and more medically appropriate too.

Drug addicts often care about only one thing—getting more of their drug of choice and obtaining it by any means at their disposal. I met one guy who sold his little sister for drugs. But by talking to former addicts who had legitimate chronic pain, I learned a lot about drug addiction, including their tricks of the trade. If you will just talk to people, they will educate you. Drug addiction occurs when a person loses sight of family and employment and destroys their world in the name of eating pills or taking substances like Tic Tacs in a bid to escape their miserable existence. I still have patients who did drugs in the sixties who use the phrase "eat my pill." I will usually interrupt them mid-sentence to tell them I understand what they mean, but they must never say that today in a world obsessed with the opioid crisis. It will always be interpreted as it sounds. I tell them that they take medications, they do not eat drugs.

Another bottom line: people are not just patients. They also need friendship, especially a non-judgmental friend. We are not treating a symptom or a disease. We need to treat the whole person. That's why I always spend more time with patients than the business of medicine wants me to. I need to know who they are before I can help them. I recall seeing a patient—a truck driver who had had his leg amputated above the knee. It wasn't mentioned anywhere on his chart. He had a prosthesis but did not walk normally. Again, no mention of his irregular gait, the accident, or when it occurred. I added this very important history to his record immediately.

I may be retired, but if anyone asks, I tell them I'm semi-retired. I still help everywhere I can. I recall a doctor who did pain management. The FBI planted agents in the parking lot outside his office, where they timed how long it took for a patient to leave his car, go into the office, and come back to his car with a prescription. They accused the doctor of running a "pill mill," meaning the patient "orders up" their medication like fast food, getting any prescription they desire. The Department of Justice filed charges, and in 2020, he lost his ability to prescribe Schedule II drugs—narcotics. He could still prescribe Schedule III drugs, so to control their pain with weaker medications, he had to prescribe higher amounts.

I was asked to mentor or counsel him by reviewing his office notes and processes when seeing his pain management patients. I also saw many of his patients in my practice when his restrictions were put into place. So, was he running a pill mill? Absolutely not. The problem was primarily in his documentation and the organization of the electronic records. The facts were in the computer but did not always appear within each progress note as they should have. When he first started referring patients to me, he would send records that I struggled to follow. It took a while before I understood his notes in the non-standard form. He was an engineer by training before entering medical school, and engineers compartmentalize facts to avoid repetition. He would put past medical history in a box, his discussion about the risk of these medications in a box, and any other issues in another box. He relied on his software, which pulled up his progress notes, to blend it all together. It was hard to sort them out, but when I finally did, I had a better understanding of the patient's current history and problems, not just a list of diagnoses, which was how it appeared with several duplications.

"You can't do that," I repeatedly explained to him. "Each time you see a patient, the visit should read like a short version of *Moby Dick*, with each progress note telling their life story and repeating vital information about drug abuse and counseling. Then, in the event someone unfamiliar with your process audits your records, they will get the full picture."

Audits of charts dealing with pain management seem to be reviewed much more frequently due to the media portrayal of the opioid crisis, which is drug abuse almost entirely. Chart audits are initially performed by nurses, who then report to a supervisory physician, who may or may not review them personally. This doctor, who had been doing well with pain management, was brilliant, with great book smarts, but it took him a while to grasp the concept with his records.

Audits of charts need to change. I believe that with today's use of electronic records, we need a new approach. Audits should include the entire computer record, not just faxed copies of progress notes from office visits, as is currently the case. Unfortunately, with many different EMRs (Electronic Medical Records) in use, no standards yet exist for consistency. Instead, they vary in setup and how they categorize clinical information. The better EMR products are costly to set up and maintain, leaving solo practices just getting by but not yet thriving without a high-quality record.

Two years after the doctor's investigation, the Department of Justice dropped the charges with no explanation, but he was still not allowed to do pain management. That decision resulted in only one outcome: more patients needlessly suffering.

He jumped through every hoop they placed in front of him, including a year of mentoring, but the Drug Enforcement Administration (DEA) continued to follow all his prescriptions. His attorney finally contacted a local DEA agent in the state who said, "We're never going to give him privileges to prescribe Schedule II drugs because he's using a lot of Schedule III drugs."

They didn't take into account that the only reason he was using Schedule III was due to his restrictions on Schedule II. His frustration eventually led this talented, intelligent, and empathetic doctor to say, "I'm done."

I don't know what his patients are going to do. The problem was never the doctor—it was the system.

Nobody looked at the full documentation of each patient's facts and risk assessment logged on his computer in that neat little box that was not visible. It just wasn't exactly where it should have been—in each progress note for each visit. The system does not look at the big picture or the whole patient because it has no written standards regarding what should be done for the use of opiate medications. Our licensure board told me they don't put standards into place for pain since it would appear they were telling doctors how to practice medicine, yet punishment is justified as not meeting a standard of care, by whose standard?

We have a Prescription Monitoring Program (PMP), which allows you to keep track of a person's prescribed controlled substances from any provider with DEA certification. When a person dies unexpectedly, and an autopsy is performed with toxicology showing an opiate or large quantity of any medication, it is officially labeled as an accidental death if the medication data from toxicology is above zero (none). Because there are therapeutic levels or ranges for medicines, these ranges should be utilized to determine if a medication prescribed was taken correctly or if there was an overdose. The reality is that in most overdose cases, the substance taken is usually an illicit drug and clearly is the cause of death with very obvious levels present. Death is actually dependent on how much narcotic, and the word overdose fits perfectly.

People rarely die taking medication as prescribed, even at higher doses. Chronic pain management patients are told that we start low and go slow with pain medications. Overdose means they either took it for the wrong reason or took it for fun. Some people think taking more medication will make the pain go away. In a sense, they're right, but the desire to take pain away too often leads to death. That is why counseling and education should never be hurried and should be done in a non-accusatory fashion.

I have had an outside job since 2004 with a life insurance company reviewing the deaths of insured patients. During that time, I have evaluated hundreds and probably thousands of Medical Examiner reports for "Cause of Death"—many are drug overdoses and many are traumatic. Becoming familiar with the toxic levels of drugs as well as ethanol levels has been eye-opening.

In the majority of overdose deaths, it seems that whenever a drug level is found, the death is ruled as due to illicit drugs without taking into account prescribed medications. There is an opioid crisis, the most obvious culprit being illicit opiates higher than the prescribed or therapeutic dose. Fortunately, since fentanyl is the popular drug in overdoses, it is possible to detect illicit fentanyl versus pharmaceutical fentanyl. If the drug is produced in a bathtub (cartel or street production), an ingredient found in the toxicology report indicates it is not pharmaceutical fentanyl. But the label on the Certificate of Death calls them accidental because society has defined an accidental death as a death that is preventable.

I would like to change the system because it's the right thing to do. Recently, the state of Oklahoma created an Overdose Committee to review all drug overdoses reported by the medical examiner's office, but no further information has emerged from this committee. I would like to be a participant in it due to my experience, but the governor appoints the members and it appears his friends in his hometown of Tulsa are the chosen ones. Maybe in the future...

When you talk to doctors about pain medications, they believe they know all they need to based on what they were taught in medical school. However, they don't understand this simple approach because medical education only discusses and focuses on the issues of addiction and abuse. Yes, there is a problem with drug abuse. I would never deny that. But I have a medical history to draw from, and I lived with chronic pain. For thirty-four years, I've learned from my hospice experience of caring for end-of-life pain issues. I have also taken the initiative to learn how to correctly treat chronic pain issues with opiate medications. Fortunately, my expected pain from past surgeries did resolve, but the unexpected and not-so-obvious trauma from nearly bleeding out due to the effect it had on my peripheral nerves with microscopic circulation has persisted.

I was blessed to have Karen at my side. Every day, she and some of my colleagues saw how frustrated I became when the pain made simple, everyday tasks difficult. Once the pain became somewhat controlled with medications, I realized I did not like the person daily pain had created. I was not very nice and far less easygoing. Then, because I took pain medications regularly, I was forced to go through the formal process of proving I was not impaired. But, the Talbot Center in Atlanta taught me one of my greatest lessons: to listen to the patient, gather the facts in my own life through open discussion with my wife, and believe in myself. That was the right way to truth.

Dr. Murray has been my hero through the thirty years he cared for me as his patient, through the good times and bad. Returning from Atlanta, we followed up and talked about being forced to go to the Talbot Center. He reaffirmed me simply by saying, "I never saw anything that would indicate impairment." He assumed the job of managing my pain, accepting me and my explanation of events. In another supportive gesture, he sent his patients to me for hospice care as well as chronic pain people. He always called me, giving me a full patient history. Receiving patients from him and other colleagues was the greatest of compliments.

Many doctors have referred chronic pain patients to me, especially in the last five to ten years of my practice. I remember one patient who voiced dissatisfaction with her primary care physician because she would pray with her while providing routine care but would not deal with her pain to the extent I did. I loved that little lady whose pain was easy to manage, leaving us time to visit and laugh about so many things in life.

I have seen overdoses over the years, but not with any of the patients I treated for pain. The latest DEA alert is for carfentanil, an elephant tranquilizer ten thousand times more potent than morphine and never meant for human consumption. One tiny grain will kill you. Unfortunately, police, along with Hollywood, have led the world to believe that anything containing fentanyl will kill you if it comes into contact with your skin. Pharmaceutical fentanyl is very useful when applied correctly as a patch, but in the real-life streets of the world, you must beware. Illicit drugs are much more dangerous than any pharmaceutical medication, and when people die, the authorities pay attention. Oddly, if someone does, people who abuse drugs will want to find the dealer who sold that specific illicit drug because clearly, it's more potent and, therefore, better. Potent? Yes. Maybe. But the user also knew how to cut the drug safely (they thought). That little fact is something I learned from reformed addicts who sometimes also have significant chronic pain, which also deserves skillful management.

We had an episode in Oklahoma City where seven young people died from the same batch of "heroin" that turned out to be fentanyl. That was what killed them. One of my chronic pain patients of many years was the mother of one of the seven, and she brought the medical examiner's toxicology report to me. It was a tragic death, and the last I heard, they were on the trail of whoever had provided the tainted drugs. That grieving mother is now raising her two grandchildren.

We still have to deal with chronic pain and drug abuse. Chronic pain is the bigger problem, but because of the attention given to drug abuse by the media, we mostly just hear their warped, inaccurate, emotional reports on the nightly news broadcasts.

CHAPTER 17

Chronic Pain - Still

I have come to believe this book may be my only forum today for expressing the importance of and approach to treating chronic pain. It seems the medical community does not want to discuss chronic pain patients. But managing pain is about quality of life, and allowing people to participate in simple activities they previously enjoyed. Treating patients with chronic pain also enables them to return to some of their less strenuous activities, bringing back to them some of the joys of life. This, coupled with improving attitudes and conditioning, is always beneficial and should always be encouraged regularly, both socially and professionally. Ignoring chronic pain can lead some people to the streets in their search for relief. People selling drugs do not care about your story; they just have a product to sell. In desperation, some people with chronic pain have gone as far as taking their own lives, some intentionally, and some due to purchasing what looked like their pain medications but were illicit drugs or even legitimate medications laced with fentanyl or carfentanil.

The issue in dealing with chronic pain is that we have no way to gauge someone else's pain objectively.

Find a good subjective tool and use it consistently with patients with interaction personally, even questioning them with subjective conflicts and objective things you notice. Pain that is present 24/7 is miserable, even if the intensity is mild. If it never goes away, it can feel like water torture, which is considered illegal in the United States under international law since it is referred to as simulated drowning. Using a pain scale with smiley faces versus frowning faces is not useful. In today's society, it seems that listening and communicating are too challenging; it appears and seems to me just easier and faster to assume every person is exaggerating their pain and, therefore, looking for drugs.

Since November 2018, doctors have frequently made the CDC guidelines their scapegoat. I believe the challenge is just to convince doctors or nurses that chronic pain actually exists since most do not experience or live with someone who lives with pain. From personal experience, I learned that accepting chronic pain is difficult. However, once I accepted my own chronic pain as irreversible, it became less frustrating and a bit easier to deal with for the last twenty-five years. Accepting it as a new reality can be tough, but that is where communication with a realistic physician can make a huge difference.

Treating pain patients kept me busy and, therefore, more distracted from my own pain, and most of my patients made me feel fortunate because, many times, their pain was more intense than mine. But I also had days of unpredictable pain. Just remember everyone has good and bad days for a variety of reasons. However, we can improve but not resolve chronic pain.

We also have to remember that healthcare undergoes medical advances and breakthroughs, so it's a good idea to keep an open mind and try to stay up-to-date with research. By the time the media reports on medical breakthroughs, it is premature, or it is no longer new news to the medical community. I also keep in mind what my grandmother always said, and that is, "If it sounds too good to be true it probably is not true." But even today, I am the person who digs through the manure looking for that pony.

The bottom line is that chronic pain patients want a magic pill or procedure that will take their pain away completely. In most cases, that is not feasible, yet some patients have operations repeatedly in hopes they will work and take away the pain that took years to develop. Also, keep in mind that by the time these chronic patients come to my office, many attempts have already been made to ease their pain unsuccessfully. One of the questions I would ask patients who knew me, along with my strange sense of humor, "Do you know what I am going to do when they come up with a magic pill to make us feel like a teenager again?"

They would look at me expectantly, and then I would say, "I will not share any of the magic pills out there!"

Many eyes would roll, followed by laughter.

One patient in her late eighties told me she'd had her toe operated on four times, yet she was willing to undergo a fifth and similar operation. I asked her why she would do that again. After four operations, nothing had essentially changed. She paused and thought about what I had asked her. Finally, she was willing to listen regarding medications to control her pain. She needed to hear someone say, "This will not take the pain away. Let's manage the pain as best we can, or at least try to improve your quality of life."

Another important consideration for chronic pain: don't write a prescription that says, "as needed." Patients may see "as needed" as a justification to take more because they still have pain. Write the prescription based on the medication's half-life, and tell the patient to take it around the clock so the level of medication in their bloodstream evens out and stays somewhat consistent over a twenty-four-hour timeframe. I always explained to take medications (not drugs) at 6, 12, 6, 12, or as close to that as possible.

Immediate-release medication has a half-life of about six hours, while extended-release medications supposedly have a half-life of twelve hours, but sometimes it is only eight hours. (Clinical pearl: rapid metabolizers, which thirty to forty percent of patients are in that group. Rapid metabolizers may require dosing every eight hours, but you should never dose extended-release medications at six hours.)

You should always discuss a patient's quality of life, which is difficult during a ten or fifteen-minute office visit. Their mood and objective observations will often give a good indication of improvement in quality. The patient walking toward the exam room normally exhibits objective behavior indicative of better pain control. This is a worthy mention in your clinical notes. Also of note, if they do not grimace during a conversation (pain is below a 7 out of 10 since grimace occurs at a seven). I frequently ask each patient, "When was the last time you had a day with no pain?"

They usually laugh because they can't remember a pain-free day, and the pain score should be based on how they have been feeling since their last visit, not on the exact minute you ask. Make sure your staff uses the same approach when asking about their pain level. You never know what each person has been through just minutes before their visit or over their lifetime.

Emotions can also have a dramatic impact on pain levels, and you have to take that into consideration. Also, if they had a family member who died of an overdose, they will blame the drug, which helps their grieving because it deflects blame from their loved one.

Chronic pain patients want respect and dignity. With repetition being the key to learning, they must be told multiple times that we all have good and bad days. Plus, after a certain age, we all have pain.

I had a patient who came for his first consultation visit and insisted all he wanted was a medical marijuana card because he was convinced it was going to take away his pain. We discussed pain control with medications, and he became frustrated until I told him I would sign his form for medical marijuana. After all, he was insistent, and it had recently been signed into law in Oklahoma, so why not give it a try? But I could not understand why he was so convinced medical marijuana would magically work. After all, he was smart and well-educated with advanced degrees, including a Law Degree.

A few months later, when his pain persisted, he was able to finally share his story with me. He wept as he told me his son had overdosed on recreational opioid drugs and died.

Eventually, we started with a low dose of pain medications that he found somewhat helpful. He shared with me how disappointed he had been when the cannabis had only helped his sleep and not his pain. Then, when COVID hit, he started working from home and his activity level went to nearly zero. As he became sedentary, he gained a lot of weight, climbing up to three hundred pounds. Not surprisingly, his emotional and physical pain intensified. His challenges were real, but together, we worked on both his issues. Walking daily will help both the weight and the emotional pain, as proven by medical studies as well.

We have to stop treating people like addicts, even those who did some stupid things in their younger years. Everyone was foolish when they were young and in college—all except me, of course. I never drove too fast in my car or on my motorcycle. At least, that's my story, and I am sticking to it. Forgive their younger transgressions; don't hold them over their head for leverage like society seems to do when we all change with age and experience.

There are addicts smart enough to make or cook up fentanyl but do not take it. They're motivated by greed, which does not make them that much different from society in general, the difference being there are legal issues with fentanyl and drugs in general, but drugs and medications are different when it comes to pain.

If we improve and perform better management of chronic pain, fewer people potentially would be overdosing and dying and doing foolish things while impaired. With correct and appropriate management of pain, fewer people may be seeking "anything for relief" in a desperate bid to reduce pain. Unfortunately, they may end up helping dealers and manufacturers get rich when they reach a desperate state of mind. Look-alike drug production is a dangerous game for the suffering population, and the unscrupulous factions in the world seem to develop better ways of manufacturing look-alikes every day.

In the Oklahoma opiate trial in 2019, where Johnson & Johnson was accused of having intentionally played down the dangers and oversold the benefits of opioids, one of the expert witnesses was a father whose son had died from an overdose. No blame was placed on anyone else in his son's life, it seemed—just the pharmaceutical company producing the legitimate medications. His son had not overdosed on a Johnson & Johnson product, but his father was put on the stand anyway. This was an emotional display of a grieving father who, in my opinion, could not be objective. His son was a very successful college athlete who likely experienced pain, but that would be true for most athletes at that level of competition. Certainly, the father's bias was fueled by love and loss. I understood because I know what it's like to lose people you care about, as well as competitive pain.

But nobody forced his son to take drugs that were likely obtained from an illicit source since they were not prescribed by a physician. The father has now dedicated his life to reducing drug abuse. He should be commended for that, but attacking the pharmaceutical industry that manufactures legitimate products should not be part of that battle, in my opinion. They are not to blame. They manufacture products intended to reduce suffering when used correctly and by appropriately trained professionals. Suing them will not impact the illicit drugs circulated and sometimes produced by drug cartels being sold by the underworld.

The underworld people have a shortened life span merely due to their participation, but the DEA reports that for each one taken off the street, there is someone else willing to jump into their place since there is a huge potential financial risk and reward.

A family member, unless specifically qualified, should not have been an expert witness. The treatment of chronic pain is affected by laws that make no sense because the media puts on an emotional display in an effort to push up ratings. Drugs do cause deaths, but how is it right to blame the manufacturers of legitimate drugs when people are dying from illicit drugs produced by greedy criminals?

I have seen people who are dying and referred to hospice at the last minute with pain out of control because doctors are afraid to get involved, not understanding what they can or cannot do due to irrational fear. If doctors can go to prison for prescribing pain medications, then something is terribly wrong. Only corrupt doctors end up in prison, not those who truly display caring and compassion along with supported by appropriate oversight and documentation. A recent Supreme Court ruling stated that the Department of Justice cannot prosecute a doctor for running a pill mill unless the doctor has shown criminal intent—a very good ruling that has reversed the punishment of some wrongfully accused doctors.

Every person training to become a physician should be educated about the correct use of opiates along with all medications. That is still not the case today in terms of opiates. *In Pain* is an excellent book by Travis Rieder, a bioethicist at Harvard Medical School who wrote about his personal experience with pain and opiates following a motor scooter accident where he nearly lost his leg. The book was published in 2019 and was given to me by one of my pain management patients. Every physician should read it.

I just want people to be treated fairly. The bitterness I felt from having to prove I was not impaired is long gone. The experience taught me so much about objectivity and communicating by listening and taking a thorough history. We were taught that this should be the first step towards treating all patients, a complete history and physical. Every personal medical adventure I have lived through has benefited me, helping me become a better doctor and a better human being. Thinking about my cancer, my leukemia, sepsis, the negative treatment by society for having pain, and caring for the terminally ill—these are precious memories nobody can take away or destroy. I used to say, "I wouldn't wish this on anybody." Today, there are probably a few people I would wish it upon, not vindictively, but to help them be more empathetic and understanding.

Not long ago, a neurologist friend was diagnosed with esophageal cancer, although his was far more advanced than mine. He had a lot of questions for me when I ran into him following his treatments, which were very different experiences from mine. Based on my own experience, I took the time to answer every one as best I could. I have had more than one doctor ask me to talk to their patients with esophageal cancer. I always say yes. The neurologist was only under my care with hospice at the very end, after fighting hard for a year or more. I will never forget him.

The important thing we should never lose sight of is whether it will be helping the patient. Always be sure to look if the considered option is legal; why not at least give the option a trial and do it? If you don't have experience with something, seek out someone who will help and learn from them. I am committed to helping as long as I am physically able.

One night, I got a call from my friend and colleague, Dr. Bill Cook, a master of pulmonary medicine. "Steve," he said, "Will you see a patient?"

"Sure."

The patient had had a heart transplant five or six years earlier and done well, but he was now running out of time. The staff, Dr. Bill Cook, the patient, and his wife had been talking about the ventilator and his wishes to discontinue the support. The patient was very spiritual and knew he had a place in heaven. He also knew the ventilator was the only thing keeping him alive, and he was tired of just existing in the Intensive Care Unit. I talked to him and his wife and explained the process of extubating him and removing the ventilator, and he said he was ready. His wife, who loved her husband very much, agreed with his wishes completely. They were both ready. I had gone back to the nurses' station located about ten feet from the room to do some paperwork and write the orders when his wife approached me and asked, "Dr. Drabek, would it be okay if I laid down in the bed with him?"

"Absolutely," I said.

How incredibly sad that she was afraid it might not be allowed.

She crawled up in bed with him. He put his arms around her. There was no real protocol for this, but I told him, as I did all my patients in his position or removing life support, that if he experienced any symptom indicating suffering or discomfort, I would address it immediately, usually with intravenous morphine or anxiety medication.

But before giving those medications, when the patients were usually not alert, I always said to any family present, "I want you to know this is the most compassionate and loving thing a family can do for their loved one." And I praised them for that support and love.

The nurses prepared as we gathered around the bed of this wonderful man with his bride lying at his side, embraced by the patient. We medicated him lightly, using a small amount of morphine to take the edge off pulling his breathing tube, thus taking away his ventilator support. Taking a few breaths, he passed with pride, dignity, and honor. He actually was looking up to God, who I'm assured welcomed him with fanfare, as he took his final breath.,

Stories like that remind me why I have a passion for hospice and that all deaths should be as wonderful as that one. He was a huge human (person) who deserved to make his own call in the end. Death is similar to birth, and the honor of being present for death should be the norm, especially when it's such a pleasant and honorable experience.

Unfortunately, in medicine, it's an anomaly—just like me—an anomaly, and I am damned proud of it as well as what I do professionally. I have had some of the most wonderful patients over my forty years of medicine, making me the luckiest person in the world. I believe every physician should be present at the bedside when death occurs if only to realize that pain and suffering have ended and they have been given what I have always referred to as a "Celestial Discharge."

One of my biggest honors and proudest moments came in 2017 when the Oklahoma Nurses Association presented me with a plaque: the Friend of Nursing Award. Following the brief ceremony, the first person with whom I shared the award on the drive home that day was my guardian angel, who began her shift as my angel on October 8, 1963.

Flora Mae Drabek RN RIP November 21, 1926 - October 8, 1963

The Road From Here

I've done a lot of reflecting while writing this book, and now I've come to the end, and I ask myself, "Where do I go from here?" (I am not done.)

I don't know. I'm not one to do a lot of planning. I'm more comfortable following my heart, and happily, it hasn't led me astray—not yet. I always say I follow my gut, which is right behind my heart since 1987 anyway.

I know I have more things to do and more challenges to meet before I head into the big unknown. After all my experience with hospice and with people suffering from chronic pain, I know what I don't want to experience at the end—PAIN.

When people came to the Hospice House, it was usually for hours or days—rarely for weeks. Regardless, the family would always ask, "How much time do we have?"

Of course, the answer is, "We don't know." And I'd tell them, "We'll get a better idea over the next few days if we're lucky."

I'd get to know the family better over time, and still, every day, they would ask, "How much time do we have?"

If I knew they had a sense of humor, which I would develop over time, my answer would sometimes change. "God is the only one who knows when they will pass, and that tells us quite a bit about God."

They'd give me a raised-eyebrow look.

I would usually smile at that point, also.

"You do know what that tells us about Him, don't you?"

"Someone would usually offer an answer like, "Um—He's got the final word, final shot?"

"No. It tells us He's not married. He answers to no one."

I might even tell the patient that little joke. Invariably, it brought smiles or even chuckles. But it was more than a joke—it was also true—and a strong reinforcement of rules number one, two, and three. (1. We all Die, 2. God Decides 3. See rule number 2.)

I believe introducing humor at a time when we're "supposed" to be somber and serious in certain groups of family members is a phenomenal way to get to know people and bring honesty to a situation that is inevitable for all of us. One thing I wish for us all is to have a personal choice at the end over how that might occur.

I recall one young man named Tyler who had sarcoma, which is almost always horrific and had his right leg amputated at the hip. Despite the surgery, he was dying since it had spread extensively. He was 23 years old, the same age and name as my son, when he flew home to Oklahoma from MD Anderson Cancer Center. One of the Native American chiefs, Chickasaw, I believe, had flown him back to Oklahoma in his private jet to be near his mother.

We admitted Tyler to the Hospice House, not quite knowing what he wanted or what his family wanted or needed based on his medical records. When I asked Tyler about going home since we all knew he was approaching death, he said, "I'd rather stay here to die here than put my parents through a lot of drawn-out suffering." An unusual request when we had his pain controlled, but he knew his mother and father would be overwhelmed trying to care for his needs and grieving.

Tyler showed more love, maturity, and caring than many people twice or three times his age. He passed in the Hospice House, saving his mother from the horrific grief of watching her son deteriorate and suffer while she felt helpless in their home in rural Oklahoma.

People must speak out on their own behalf. They shouldn't rely on doctors to make their personal decisions. I want people to think about their own desires long before they are in dire condition. Yes, we all want to live, but we have to define what living is. What does quality of life mean for you? For me, it means "Blowing and going wherever and whenever with whoever I want and therefore being with the important people (and pets) in my life."

I am hopeful that we have more of these discussions and that they will change medicine, introducing compassion back where it is needed. Everyone talks about how medicine has changed, but not necessarily in a positive way. First and foremost, medicine has to be about compassion, empathy, and caring, not about "doing things" to people. We have become more skilled at prolonging death than at extending life. We must ask ourselves again, what do we want life to be about?

Modern medicine also seems to be putting profits ahead of people and is more expensive than ever. We have new equipment, new technology, and new drugs—all with skyrocketing costs. Also, couple that with the world and liability in medicine.

I think the medical world needs to change its mindset from believing it can fix everything to concentrating on making it better. And a lot of things can be made better. I've had cataract surgery and not having to wear glasses is a huge step toward improving my life. But there are also too many physicians who perform the same steps on everyone based on what they've been taught to do and what generally works. But trying to get medicine to go back to the days of *Marcus Welby* is never going to happen.

What was it about that old TV show that had people tuning in every week? It aired from September 23, 1969, to May 4, 1976, starring Robert Young as the title character, a family practitioner with a kind bedside manner who made house calls and was on a first-name basis with many of his patients. He had empathy, something you simply can't teach, but we have no trouble recognizing it. It's that warm fuzzy feeling that makes us tingle or even weep sometimes, leaving us with the desire to experience it again and again.

Karen tells me I suffer from "empathy overload," and I think that's probably spot on because I have been in my patients' shoes. I've had chronic pain for years. I have chronic leukemia. And I've had a life-changing operation. I know how my patients feel.

Pain doesn't show up on an MRI scan or a CT Scan, or, as I often told patients, "We can do an autopsy, but it probably won't show anything that gives us a definitive answer." Pain does not reveal itself in all our standard tests. The medical community sometimes thinks it has all the answers, and it has come up with some brilliant ones, like the polio vaccine or the lifesaving treatment for AIDS, but we still don't give chronic pain enough attention, and we certainly can't eliminate death.

I have so many stories. I could write an entire book based only on the stories of my patients. I've been blessed to develop meaningful relationships with many of them, and perhaps that's the high point of my long medical career. Some of those connections were with people who had profound issues, while others had simple problems we could easily solve.

As a physician, I have been honored to have people share with me some of their most human fears, hopes, and stories. Being able to help them has made this career worthwhile. I am proud to be known as a comfortologist. What I found over the years is that when people came to the Hospice House, they didn't need to hear about their hypertensive-this or their metastatic-that; they needed to hear about it in a different language. I called it "medical translation." They needed comfort, so putting things in layman's terms for simplification defines the medical translation.

If I could change the medical community, I would put far more focus on compassion, caring, and pain relief. It all comes down to empathetic listening and giving a damn about the person, not the prestige or finding a Nobel-prize-winning cure. It's about making someone's life better, making them smile, or better yet, letting out a belly laugh or cackle.

Maybe that's the unplanned road I have yet to travel: continue offering comfort, being empathetic and caring, and always, always doing my best to make people's lives better.

Dorothy from The Wizard of Oz was correct: "There is no place like home."

That is most hospice experiences in the home; please think of it when needed.

God willing, (wink) to be continued...

Acknowledgments

Praise and acknowledgment go to the "Big Guy" first. He was the one who led me through my sometimes treacherous but highly rewarding journey, demonstrating the power He possesses as well as the faith required to withstand whatever came my way. He constantly winked at me by providing me with the safe and rewarding path called life. He gave me a beautiful family as well as opportunities in a career I was born to fulfill.

Thanks to my Guardian Angel, my mother, who left behind a legacy of compassion when she departed her earthly life in 1963. This compassion led me to develop and embrace an empathetic approach to my patients, enabling me to develop my passion for the rewards of end-of-life care by reducing the suffering of patients and giving them a better quality of life. I was able to enhance my God-given skills using personal experiential learning along with my quirky sense of humor.

Thanks to James Bearden, M.D., who taught me to focus on the importance of looking for an answer and then delivering the message, no matter how difficult, because, in the end, the truth allows for acceptance and enables us to move forward, always doing the best we can. (Rule#2: God decides when it is over.)

Don Murray, M.D., saved my life despite my naivety, which prevented me from seeing the danger in my personal illnesses. Thank you for always standing by me, knowing the truth, and understanding my drive for compassion and honesty, which may be a difficult choice in today's medical community. He also taught me that sometimes there is no absolute definitive answer, and it is okay to admit not knowing. He was willing to admit that simple fact, but always and only after searching diligently for an answer.

Thanks to Brian Geister, M.D., for being willing to care for his controversial colleague and friend and for sending his patients to me when their need for personal care at the end of life required a unique approach. Thank you for teaching me it is okay to be excited about medical science as a young student hungry for knowledge. Through laughter and compassion at challenging times, he showed me that the best approach might be through empathy and caring as well as honesty and seriousness when it really counts.

Karen showed me love, unconditional support, and, at times, advocacy and protection, even when I didn't think I deserved it. My children, Madison and Tyler, instilled a drive to go on and provide for their needs. I only wish I had been less distant at times. Karen, Tyler, and Madison taught me the meaning of family. Over the years, the family dogs have given me unconditional devotion, always accepting my sometimes-challenging moods. Now, in semi-retirement, Otis P my rescued Pit/Boxer mix, helped me rehabilitate my lungs after COVID. He also trained me well to meet his need and desire for bacon treats. When it comes time for Otis to cross the rainbow bridge, I will go through an intense grieving experience, but I am reminded of the "pack" that will meet me on the other side. And that is because all dogs go to heaven.

Special thanks to SQuire Rushnell for providing me with the explanation of the events that made up my life with the concept of GOD WINKS. When I present people with a copy of your first book, I explain that it would be hard to make some of this stuff up. I am sure my family has heard me talk about your book so often they could tell the stories from memory.

I must not forget, Dr. William Spencer Payne at the Mayo Clinic with his expertise, surgical skills, and passion for esophageal diseases and surgery of the esophagus. Dr. Payne is the reason I'm sitting here writing about my medical highlights, with my career beginning three months later in Yukon, Oklahoma. He removed my small cancerous lesion by taking my entire esophagus with half of the stomach, and it saved me. Dr. Payne passed in 1999. He was a very empathetic surgeon who always returned my calls and answered my questions. Thank You, Dr. Payne and the Mayo Clinic, for your care and my survival.

I also wish to thank Authors on Mission for their support and encouragement in helping me complete this book, a project so important to me. I will share it with pride.

Also, a well-deserved thank you to my fellow residents, faculty, and staff at the Tulsa Medical College Family Medicine program in 1987 for the assistance they provided to Karen and me in those final months of residency training and for making recovery from surgery and finishing up my residency tolerable and enjoyable.

Finally, to all the patients who brought joy and sorrow, I say THANK YOU.

About the Author

Dr. Steve Drabek and his wife, Karen, live in Yukon, Oklahoma, with their dog, Dog Otis P., and Karen's huskies, Mia and Jasmine. They have two children, Madison and Tyler, and a daughter-in-law, Jackie. Dr. Drabek semi-retired in mid-2023 but remains committed to supporting hospice and palliative medicine patients.

Born in 1956, he graduated from the University of Oklahoma Health Sciences Center in 1984. Following medical school, he moved to Tulsa for a three-year family medicine residency. He has been certified in family medicine since 1987, returning to the Oklahoma City area and settling in Yukon. His interest in end-of-life care came early when he authored a story, *The Incredible Smile,* published in the Oklahoma State Medical Association Journal in 1984. He was certified in hospice and palliative medicine in 2000-2015.

He has a lifelong passion for caring for underserved populations of medical service.

You can contact Dr. Drabek on Facebook at stevedrabekmd or on his website, SteveDrabekMD.com.